Down Memory Lane

Down Memory Lane

Compiled by Joscelyne V.C. Turner

Platt Memorial Hall
2016

First Printing: 1984
Second Printing: 2016

ISBN 978-1-326-65201-2

Platt Memorial Hall
Platinum Way
Platt, Sevenoaks, Kent, TN15 8FH

www.plattmemorialhall.org

Down Memory Lane has been reprinted to mark the closure of the first Platt War Memorial Hall, which was built in 1922, and to celebrate the opening of the new building on 3rd September 2016.

CONTENTS

ACKNOWLEDGMENTS

I wish to thank the following: Shiela Goodworth for all typing. Brian Hulme for preparation and reproduction of the map of Platt 1860 by Mary Anne Kunkel. Leonard Harmsworth for map of Wrotham Heath 1820. Kenneth Browne for permission to reproduce his drawing of 'The Blue Anchor.' Freda Cross for the opportunity to study a copy of 'The Free Traders' by the late John Terry, pub. 1888. Keith Denham of Ford Place, Wrotham Heath, for access to Deeds and papers in connection with Platt Mill. My daughter Mary Anne Kunkel, for the sketches of Platt Woods. Those who have contributed their memoirs and lent photographs, and to Dick Hollands who suggested the title 'Down Memory Lane.' Sue Vinson for sketch "A house in the Woods" and Susan Hulme for map of Platt 1568

Compiled by Joscelyne V.C. Turner, 1984

This reprint was produced by kind permission of Joscelyne Turner's family. We are very grateful to Peter Geliot and also Lucilla Mackay, who carefully transcribed the text from the original manuscripts. Barry Baker provided digitised copies of the photographs, and Scott Wishart, who also photographed and designed the cover, reformatted the book for publication.

Platt Memorial Hall, 2016

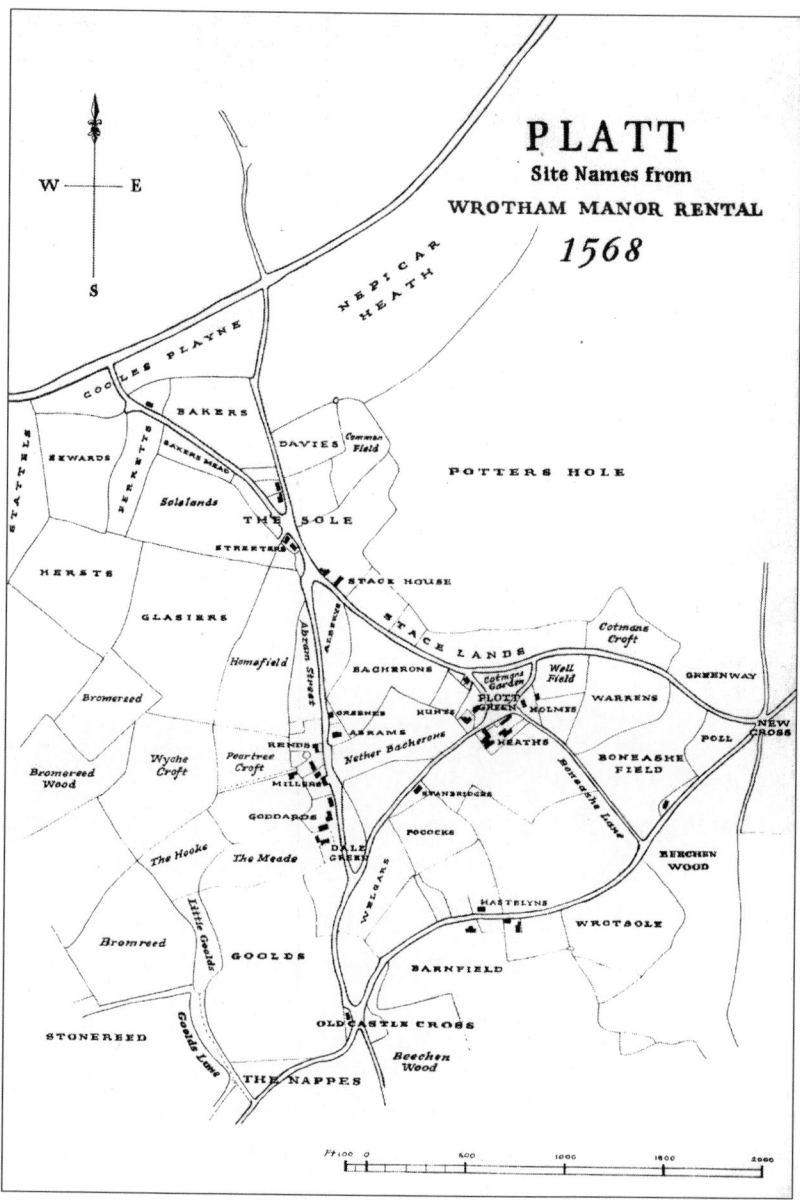

PLATT

Site Names from

WROTHAM MANOR RENTAL

1568

W — E
S

NEPICAR HEATH

COOLES PLAYNE

BAKERS

DAVIES

Common Field

POTTERS HOLE

STATTLES

BAKERS MEAD

SEWARDS

Solelands

THE SOLE

STREETERS

STACK HOUSE

HERSTS

GLASIERS

STACE LANDS

Cotmans Croft

Homefield

Abrams Street

BACHERONS

Well Field

GREENWAY

Bromereed

Cotmans Garden

FLOUD GREEN

WARRENS

GREENERS

HUNTS

HOLMES

NEW CROSS

ABRAMS

HEATHS

POLL

Wyche Croft

Peartree Croft

RENDS

Nether Bacherons

BONEASHE FIELD

Bromereed Wood

MILLERS

Boneashe Lane

GODDARDS

SPANBRIDGES

The Hooke

DALE GREEN

POCOCKS

BEECHEN WOOD

The Meade

WELGARS

Little Goulds

HASTELYNS

WROTSOLE

Bromreed

GOOLDS

BARNFIELD

STONEREED

Goulds Lane

OLD CASTLE CROSS

Beechen Wood

THE NAPPES

Ft.100   0   500   1000   1500   2000

1

ST MARY PLATT NATIONAL SCHOOL 1847 - 1912

J.V.C. Turner

Up to the early years of this century, education had been chequered by religious feuds and intolerance. The Church of England created The National Schools Society in 1811 – Non-Conformists and Dissenters 1807 called their schools The British and Foreign School Society. The British School in Platt was held in a house now called Foxbury, where boarders as well as day pupils attended at a higher fee (Benjamin Harrison walked daily from Ightham to this school).

When John Mickleburgh became the first Vicar of Platt, indeed, immediately after his "Institution" as it was then called, he set about making plans for a school to be known as Platt National School. In February 1846, together with his Churchwarden Captain Randolph of Great Comp, they met their Architect Whichcord on the proposed site (16 rods bounded on three sides by Glebe Land, and a road on the South West just below the Church) when Tomlyn's (the builder) estimate of £640 was accepted. This sum was raised by public subscription, which included a gift of £150 from the family of the late Rector of Wrotham, the Reverend George Moore, plus grants from the Government and National Society. By the summer of that year the foundations were completed, and at a cost of 2/6 the first stone was laid. Scarcely had six months elapsed than John Mickleburgh rode to Great Comp to settle with Captain Randolph about school books, materials and equipment, for which the Vicar was responsible, and he was soon ready to receive applications for pupils.

Mr. and Mrs. Perkins and pupils 1890

"The School is for the education of the labouring, manufacturing and other poorer classes in the Chapelry District... in union with and conducted upon the principles and in furtherance of the ends and designs of the Incorporated Society for promoting the Education of the poor in the principles of the Established Church",

which is why John Mickleburgh called his creation "The National School". This school opened in 1847 with fifty pupils under a Mr. Crittle from Ightham as Headmaster, whose salary was 10/- per week, plus the children's pence, parents paying 1d per week for each child, bringing the total to 14/2 and a house, now called St. Mary's Lodge. An inscription on a tombstone in Platt Churchyard reads:

'Daniel Shelven, died August 1861 aged 31, having been National School Master in this Parish for thirteen years'

According to Kelly's Directory of 1874, the Mistress was a Mrs. Bonaker, succeeded in 1883 by Mr. F. Perkins, and it was to him that pupils, provided with a Coal Card, brought the sum of not less than 8d per month, which entitled their parents to coal at 19/6 per ton. They could also join the Clothing Club paying at least 4d per month – these subscriptions were supplemented by local Benefactors.

"Education is now free and compulsory, but this is no reason why those who excel in diligence, good behaviour and in regular attendance, should not be encouraged by receiving prizes. Children are given to parents to train and not in order that their little hands and feet should be put at a very early age to the strain of hard work, that will come soon enough, and well-educated children are less likely to grow into idle and discontented men and women".

In March 1899, H.M. Inspector examined the school, and in the following month, the Diocesan Inspector was expected to examine the children in Religious Knowledge. Special prizes were given by Capt. and Mrs. Smith of Basted, one to a girl for needlework, won by Bertha Luck, and one to a boy won by F.T.C. Broad both for regular attendance and good conduct. Prizes for never being absent from school the previous year were won by F.T.C. Broad, Kate Bartholomew, Rose, Ernest and Florence Hogben, Emily Taylor, George and John Bance, Phoebe Byne and Daisy Sands. In July 1900, on behalf of Mr. and Mrs. Terry of The Grange, each child was presented with a pocket handkerchief bearing on it the portrait of a soldier serving in the Boer War.

In 1900 the Headmaster was Mr. Dover, a harsh disciplinarian, complaints of whose caning of small pupils was reported. His salary was £120 per annum, that of his wife who also taught, £75, an assistant Miss Annie Perkins £50.

In 1910 owing to over-crowding and inadequate premises, there was a proposal to sell the school building, although considerable improvements had been made, when a portion of the large school-room was re-floored, made brighter by means of paint and varnish, and the introduction of match-boarding to a portion of the walls, and the girls' cloakroom was re-floored. It was suggested to build a larger school on Glebe Land. However, on January 11th 1912 a new school was proposed at a cost of £650, plus £150 for a

Mr Dover & Class in 1908

shelter and shed, though the exact site is not given in the School
Minutes. On March 13th of that year, Miss Bright from Worthing
Hill School, Pevensey, and her Assistant, Miss Shrubb were
interviewed and appointed as Headmistress and Sub Mistress
assisted by a Miss Pottle, and from that time on, the school became
an Elementary School, now Platt Primary, Church of England
School, situated in Sandy Lane (Platt Common).

Note (According to Mr. Stanley Box)

On leaving school during Mr. Dover's headmastership each pupil was presented with a card bearing these words:-

> *His last work for his scholars done,*
> *He says his usual prayer.*
> *God bless and guard you everyone*
> *The children in my care.*
> *With many thoughts and bitter pain*
> *Follows this prayer tonight.*
> *God bless and guard you everyone*
> *The children in my sight.*

With a loving God bless you from Arthur J. Dover.

"THE MARCH OF TIME"

John Geddes

St. MARY PLATT (as originally in the singular) has no history, indeed according to the map of 1568 (see p1) the name is PLOTT, marked where the house called "Pigeon's Green" now stands. The original hamlet, a small cluster of dwellings, is shown in the area surrounding Platt Farm. When the Church was built however, between 1841 and 1842 (the date on the weather vane of the tower 1843) and we separated from Wrotham, then this lower area became the centre of the village eventually to be called St. Mary Platt, and maps of a later date show how the local population had shifted to be near the Church.

In the meantime the cutting for the railway was being surveyed and levelled. This proved a considerable and difficult operation; the excavation work by navvies was hard, and the cuttings through Holly Bank and Gallow's Hill needed special skills as well as the building of six bridges. During this period of levelling and banking up, much of the red sand-stone was removed and used for building purposes, hence some local houses and cottages look so different from those built with Kentish rag-stone. I suggest that these workmen were

Welsh miners, some of whom settled on Platt Common in thatched huts, some in Windmill Hill, Wrotham Heath in a row called "Navvies' Cottages". So now we have Welsh names added to the local population, such as Bowen and Evans, and a Mr. Thomas of Wrotham Heath House. Two of the Miss Mansell triplets were well known ladies from North Wales, who lived in Nepicar Lodge, and with the wife of Dr. Francis Charlewood Turner of Warren Wood, were responsible for the building of the Mission Room, until recently at the bottom of Windmill Hill, where Mother's Union meetings and, other village activities took place.

Platt had its share of Irishmen, from whom we have such names as Terry, Larkins and Higgins. From Scotland came Findley, the landlord of The Royal Oak at Wrotham Heath – Geddes, Orr, farm workers, and of course the Heron-Maxwells of Gt. Comp mentioned in the November 1977 issue of the parish magazine. For the Kentish names in our locality come Hogben, Glover, Fuller, Hollands, Vidler, Thacker, Thatcher, Pierce, Ashdowne, Carter, Wolfe, Tanner and many more, all living and working in this parish, in farm work, brick and tile making, charcoal burning for hopdrying and other crafts. With the building of Whatcote in 1904, came fresh names, three of whom stayed and lived in Platt – Holness, Ladd and Lowes, which is an example of how an industry can add new names and often new ideas to a district.

Platt Woods with the oak and conifers were planted up with chestnut, a timber used for utility purposes such as fencing, hop poles, stock poles, building construction, and in the making of carts and farm carts; the old Kentish plough was made of wood shod with steel. Faggots from brush wood provided pea and bean sticks and had other uses. This area was the home of the wild life, including still a number of Badger sets. The rhododendron has taken over, but the Cedars still look magnificent, especially the Sequions [Sequoias].

Platt Woods, Nr. Borough Green.

Time in my early life was much less hectic, and for the hour we relied on the Brickyard bell, the steam horn of Basted Mill and the Church clock. To obtain the exact time one contacted the station, or asked the postman. But for the last thirty years we have been changed from truly rural serenity to an almost suburban 'what [time] is it?' Now we adjust our clocks and watches to the pips on the Radio.

RECOLLECTIONS AND REFLECTIONS

John Geddes

1, Church Villas, St. Mary Platt

I was born in Wigtownshire the eldest child of my father's second marriage. He was descended from four generations of Scottish ploughmen and like them all he was named James. My father accompanied Mr. and Mrs. Heron-Maxwell of Dun Cree (Wigtownshire) when they bought Great Comp early in this century and he became their head gardener.

At first, our family lived in Park Bungalow opposite the big house and later we moved to Gate Bungalow until 1934. The Park (now "Windmill Park") and the Leys were our playground, full of wild life, also the woods of Platt, a forest of pines where the red squirrel made his home until, with the outbreak of the First War, the trees were felled and he disappeared. The Park was heathland with heather, broom and furze; fine trees of oak, chestnut, larch, birch and one crab-apple and one walnut tree. The undergrowth teemed with wild life – mice, lizards, adders, grass snakes and the weasel who was difficult to see; his head popping up and – flash! he had gone. The skylark nested and reared its family and filled the air with its song. All the finch family was there and wagtails, flycatchers, wiverns, blackbirds, thrush and the magpie and jay who gave your presence away!

The pond on the boundary with Valley Wood was sometimes so full of water it overflowed until on August 15th 1940 a German bomb landed and exploded in the middle of it and no water has been seen since. There is a lime-kiln, a fine specimen brick-built with an iron furnace front. Today this is overgrown, but if cleared would be an asset to the garden of which it is part. "The Park" as it was called was indeed a wonderful playground for children of the district and an excellent site for the Girl Guides' summer camps which came annually from the East End of London and other places needing open space. There never was a windmill in this area, the only one being on Gallow's Hill overlooking Wrotham Heath and on a map of 1888 is marked "only used as a store-room".

The Leys, something like the Park but with more heather, had similar wild life with the addition of the pee-wit a regular visitor during Spring and Summer. It nested and reared its family in its own peculiar way uttering its haunting cry. The owl was there and the badger, also the fox with its cubs – a never-ending source of joy providing you approached quietly like a good countryman. In the Leys is a slab of concrete, a relic of the First War. It was made to hold listening apparatus to track enemy aircraft, and operators then 'phoned information to the searchlights battery situated on the Golf

Course. During our first Summer term at Platt National School, we went barefoot but were promptly sent home and told to return wearing stockings and boots. The boys wore what was called "straights" which were not shaped so they could be worn on either foot, but they were hob-nailed, hard and uncomfortable. After finishing our early education in the temporary school in Borough Green which was situated behind what is now the Clinic, we went to the newly built council school in Borough Green behind the present Barclays Bank, and which we left at 14. I was then apprenticed to Curtis and Cain but released in 1915 in order to join the R.F.C. subsequently transferred to the R.A.F. at Montrose until demobilisation when I returned to Curtis and Cain.

Then came the days of high unemployment, and so I moved around wherever there was work to be had. In 1931, I married Minnie Gower at St. Mary's Church, West Malling, then we came to Platt where we have lived ever since and where our son, Brian, was born.

I have been asked to write about Great Comp during the days of Mr. and Mrs. Patrick Heron-Maxwell who bought the property from the Hon. Ralph Nevill. It is said he would never have sold it had he known they were damn'd Liberals! Mr. Heron-Maxwell J.P. was a typical conventional country gentleman, charming and unassuming. He seldom smoked and never in the house. He was the third son of Edward Heron-Maxwell of Penningham, a large estate close to the River Cree (a staunch Liberal family). Mrs. Heron-Maxwell was the fifth daughter of Admiral Cockburn, descended from a long line of Scottish politicians and lawyers one of whom helped to draw up the Act of Union in 1707. She was a pioneer of Women's Rights, a forcible woman who amongst many other activities, started the Women's Institute in Kent and made Great Comp the headquarters of the Women's Land Army during the Second World War. She used the gymnasium for packing of uniforms.

According to Hasted, the original house of Great Comp was built about 1600 by Sir William Howe though the domestic quarters are probably Victorian additions. The front porch which is certainly not in keeping with the front elevation was probably built when the road to the north-west ran nearer to the house than now. The present road, no doubt, was made at the same time as Mereworth Lane, i.e. circa 1800. I base this date on the fact that Park Bungalow was originally the entrance lodge to the Park leading from Great Comp to Platt Common. The Victorian interior of the house was removed and the whole put back to its original Tudor grandeur. It is said that the Heron-Maxwells also completely altered the surrounding land. An orchard was started, the gardens enlarged and transformed. The adjacent Oast and its adjoining building converted into a lovely country house (now known as Lambard's Oasts) which blended in with part of the new garden. There was also a Dutch garden, a herb garden and a lily pond constructed under a mulberry tree. Three greenhouses with a boiler house and potting sheds were added; tennis courts were laid out and two hockey pitches with provision for cricket during the Summer. A gymnasium was built to act as a Club House and as a Pavillion. For a time the kitchen garden was adapted to a style called "French Gardening" under a Mr. Hayes who lived in a small thatched bungalow near Blacksmith's Wood, but the scheme had to be abandoned.

By now there was a ladies' hockey team - "The Pilgrims" - Mrs. Heron-Maxwell acting as goal-keeper; a ladies' tennis club and cricket team which later during the 20's toured Australia captained by Miss Archdale of Crouch. In fact one could now call Great Comp a women's world. In 1920 if you stood on the lawn facing South you would admire not only the scene but the thought and work which had gone into the reconstruction of this property since the Heron-Maxwells bought it. The garden stretched out in front, the fields skirting it with grazing cattle, the green of the grass, the golden corn in season and beyond, more green with a flock of sheep. Then there were the heather colours and in the Autumn the tints of the distant woodlands. All this was not by accident, for cutting and clearing had opened up this view.

From 1908 three families shared the estate - the McLarens in the Oasts; Miss Somervill in Comp Shoot and the Heron-Maxwells in the main house. All had so much in common - they were active Liberals enthusiastic in sports. Miss Somervill, although an ardent feminist, was a very gifted craftswoman and when she moved to the "Oasts", she spent much time spinning and weaving the cloth worn by the ladies (now including Miss Vera Cox) of Great Comp. Miss Somervill also started an open air theatre under a large oak tree in the north-east corner of the Park with seats on blocks of wood. She directed Shakespearian plays the actors being local people. Other dramatics took place in the gymnasium, and I am sure many of the casts are still with us.

By this time the site of the farm had been taken by the conversion of the "Oasts" so Mrs. Heron-Maxwell had other farm buildings altered and re-organised. The cow sheds (now a small concert hall), cart sheds, stables and storage space and a new dairy was attached to Miss Somervill's Oast where butter was made, milk skimmed for cream and sold direct. Some of us still remember calling there for milk and dairy produce. The Garage and the cottage at Comp Corner were built, one on the road to Offham for the chauffeur and the house on Seven Mile Lane converted into a laundry with living quarters for the staff. However the laundry was not a success so was usually taken by one of us children by pony trap to Offham. The house and out-buildings became the head gardener's house.

In 1936 Mr. Heron-Maxwell died, aged 80 at Great Comp, and his wife died in Switzerland in 1955 aged 91. So a 50 year reign ended. The big house and outbuildings have been divided and converted into separate dwellings. The garden most beautifully re-constructed by Mr. and Mrs. R. Cameron is open to view by the public during Summer months on Fridays and Sundays.

FURTHER MEMORIES OF PLATT
Nellie Hollands 1905–1979

My mother, Ellen Broad, was born in 1879 the daughter of Jonas Broad, a shepherd, living in what is now Nepicar Farm – in those days known as Nepicar Meadows. She married William Bartholomew in 1901. He lived at that time in the Mount, Borough Green, subsequently moving to what is now Orchard Place Farm where he worked for Mr. Pierce's father. Later we lived with my grandfather James Bartholomew in Vine Cottage, Platt, now called "Dales". Afterwards my father worked for Platt Mill so we moved to 6 Sobraon Villas. After I left school, amongst other employment, I worked for Pearson, the village store where bread was baked behind the shop and I helped to cut the dough which when cooked was made into bread puddings and sold at ½d per slice. I also helped Mrs. McDougall Porter (a cousin of the late Captain Turner) as kennel maid for her Alsatians which she bred at Grange Cottage on adjoining land now the site of "Crofton".

In those days Platt Church Fair was held in "Anchor Fields" now St. Mary's Close. My brother-in-law worked for Canon Mallinson as gardener, indeed I have known nine vicars: the Rev.

John Brand, Rev. John Newton, (afterwards) Canon Mallinson, Rev. A. Cross, Rev. E.L.L. McClintock, Canon R.V. Bristow, Canon R. Soar, the Rev. Victor Kingston O.B.E., and our present vicar the Rev. R.V. Douglas.

Mr. Brand owned cowsheds in the churchyard situated where the rubbish heap is now and other cowsheds on the opposite side of the path leading into the woods. We went to the Vicarage with our own jugs and bought fresh milk at 2d per quart.

In 1926 Platt Mill was burnt down – their sacks of wheat and flour were scattered leaving a dreadful smell which lasted for days.

As stated by my husband in the following memories Dick and I were married at Platt Church in 1929 and one son, Syd, was born in 1930 (over to Dick) –

Dick Hollands

I was born in 1905 in part of Rose Cottage, Platt – then two dwellings. My father, Frank Hollands, being employed by Mr. Lauser of Beechin Wood Farm. My mother, Harriett, née Fuller, was a cousin of the late Harry Fuller then resident in Porch Cottage. Of our family one daughter, Nellie, was a well-known inhabitant of Platt and four sons; Syd the eldest was killed on the eve of his 21st birthday during the first World War. Tom became the familiar and faithful postman making his twice daily round on a push-bike whatever the weather – a man still remembered with affection and esteem.

During our stay in Rose Cottage, my father witnessed the loss of a golden sovereign – a man's weekly wages – which was accidentally dropped into the apparently bottomless well in the grounds of "Oak Beams" the site of which is now covered by a mound of grass. After leaving Rose Cottage we moved to half of Kettle Cottage and in 1907 our family moved again, this time to No.3 Church Villas one of the three houses now occupied by Mrs. Hollands, Mrs. Pett and Mr. and Mrs. Geddes. These houses were built by my Fuller grandmother of "The Blue Anchor".

Our house was opened as a confectioner's shop when my father took over "The Blue Anchor" where he owned a horse and trap. I often accompanied one of my brothers on a round of the locality, which included Offham, selling amongst other items, confectionery, soft drinks, tobacco and even haberdashery. The only supply of water was obtained from a well outside the pub. This well contained amongst other things dead birds, mice and the occasional boot which did us no harm, In 1921, however, owing to severe drought the well dried up and Style and Winch, the brewers and owners were obliged to connect us to the main supply. I often found 4d on the shelf in the Bar – payment for a job awaiting me at Mr. Will Cadby's house now called "Ruffway". This house was originally built for the curate, and during Mr. and Mrs. Cadby's tenancy it was known as Platt Cottage and was afterwards occupied by Mrs. Fox, a churchwarden, and was then known as "Fox's Place".

I was in the choir under Mrs. Percy Minter of "Staddleswood" the church choir mistress (who also played the organ); we were paid by her 6/3d per quarter each, and an extra 1/- for solo singing. My wife and I were both members of the choir and early every January a choir supper was held in The Old Schools supervised by Mrs. McDoughall-Porter and her husband, Tom, who was a churchwarden.

During the first World War, Dr. Gordon Jones (whose widow, Isabel, it will be remembered, died aged 104) gave First Aid lessons to the ladies of Platt for whom I acted as a casualty being trussed up like a chicken with wooden splints and bandages.

Platt Woods were privately owned by the Nevills of Birling and Mr. Crouch was the keeper, a formidable man who allowed no one to walk through the woods except on Sunday when the path to the church was opened and gates firmly shut after Evensong by the verger, Mr. Prentice. My wife and I were at the Old Schools, Platt, together proceeding to the Church of England School now Platt Primary School where some 50 of us occupied two class-rooms. We finally finished our education in Borough Green School at the age of 14. The school was situated behind what is now Barclay's Bank, formerly a bakery. During part of school hours I worked in the neighbouring fields, cultivating vegetables for school consumption.

After leaving school I worked for Mr. Todman cultivating stock at Basted House, though my ambition to join the Police Force had to be abandoned as I did not pass the test for the required height and the fact that my father kept a tavern.

Church Road, Platt.

In 1929 I married Nellie Bartholomew in Platt Church and subsequently lived in Little Platt Cottage working for the late Mr. Godfrey Marshall. During the Second World War my wife and I acted as caretakers for the Old Schools which were requisitioned by the army as a Recreation Room for the troops stationed in this district. After Mr. and Mrs. Marshall left Platt, I worked for Mr. and

Mrs. Michael Barton of Bell Orchard. It may be of interest to know that as late as 1923 when Commander Maxwell (a churchwarden according to my copy of the Parish Magazine of that period) was dying in Stone Cottages, hay was spread on the main road by his house to deaden the noise.

"AS TOLD TO ME"

Miss Olive Gilbert

"How wonderful to get a light by just pressing a knob" said my mother (then aged 94) as I switched on the electric light one evening. "When I was very young" she continued, "we had nothing but candlelight. We had tin candlesticks with shiny reflectors which hung on the walls, and nice shiny brass ones in the parlour.

Platt was very different in those days, so quiet you could hear the birds sing. Nowadays the noise of traffic drowns their song. The roads ware narrow and stony, a horse and cart brought the stones which were put into heaps at the road-side, and a man came to break them up with a hammer. Men then came and spread them for the horses and carts to tread in, there being no steamrollers. Traffic was very light, an occasional horse, or pony-trap, a farm wagon, sometimes a carriage and pair.

My grandfather, Henry Stiles, who built the original "Brickmakers' Arms" about 1825, and my father were carriers to London before the railway came this way. Twice a week a two-horse van set out for London in the evening, loaded with hops and fruit, and other produce according to season, and brought back stores for local shops and other things required. A change of horses was kept at "The Bull" Birchwood, near Swanley, specially shod for the cobblestones of the London streets. The van would arrive at Covent Garden early next morning, and return in the evening changing horses again at Birchwood. There was a toll-gate at Borough Green, near to the present Tollgate Estate, where the driver had to pay the toll. Sometimes in order to avoid payment he would drive on through Nepicar to Wrotham Heath, and round by the Sevenoaks Road, back to Platt! Passengers were taken but an extra horse would be necessary for the long pull up Wrotham Hill.

The house now called "Foxbury" was a boys school, boarders and day pupils; a "British School" (the school room eventually became Valerie Stoner's shop). I remember standing in the field where Platt Memorial Hall is now situated, watching boys flying kites. Where "The Grange" now stands, there were two cottages, set in a cherry orchard, and I remember taking clothes to be mangled by an old man who had a big table-mangle, weighted with stones in one of those cottages. In the other lived the man who drove the cattle or sheep to and from market. Sometimes they came long distances and rested for the night in the drover's yard. I would run out to shut our gates when the cattle were passing, for if they got into the garden, it was a job to get them out again.

Brickmaker's Arms 1860
(In entrance is Ann Styles aged 10 years, mother of Olive Gilbert)

There was a man named John Terry, who left his work in the hop-garden and went to London in one of our vans; years later he returned a rich man and bought the two cottages and the land between Grange Road and Sandy Lane from the Nevill's, diverting the foot-path to High Haugh, which used to run between Grange Road at the brow of the hill to its present line now known as "Tin Pan Alley". Mr. Terry pulled down the cottages and built "The Grange", the two remaining dwellings on Grange Road being kept for his coachman and gardener. He had the cave dug which is entered from "Grottan", thought to have been a smuggler's hide-out in former days. It was a lovely walk to Borough Green, and except for "The Grange", no houses on the left with the exception of Fir

Tree Cottages and Staddleswood, country abounding in pheasants and rabbits. Then hop gardens and two oast houses with a cottage attached in which the hopdrier man lived. On the right, after "Cloggatts" were nut plantations and hop gardens down to Black Horse Farm. Only two shops in Borough Green, a butcher (now Kitney's coal merchant office) and a general store. There was no Post Office in Platt, only a post box built into the wall of the Almshouses. A small shop, Ellis's, and Mary Ellis, the daughter, would walk with me across the fields to Wrotham, taking the money to the Bank; this money was tucked into my dress and we took the dogs. Wrotham was quite an important place in those days, a Fair being held every year on May 4th.

"Mr Micawbers"

I remember, when sometime in 1880, a man named Tom Fry started up the windmill on Gallow's Hill, Wrotham Heath, which had been out of use, but one evening in 1900 it was burnt down. He also built the grain-store, later "Mr. Micawber's", the flour-mill was built by Mr. Jull. I remember about 1875 running across the field opposite to watch the first train go by. When I was young, hop gardens stretched nearly all the way from Platt to Comp, Crouch; indeed as far as Plaxtol with the occasional oast house. In the hopping season, crowds of Londoners came down to help with the picking and lived in hopper-huts, some on Stonehouse farmland at Crouch, and in Platt Yard (now Pigeon's Green). Some of these hoppers were very rough, and you had to watch out for your purse, if you went out at night.

If you walked up the Common, now Sandy Lane, in 1880, there was to be seen in a dip, a cluster of very small thatched cottages, and I remember an old man, named Smith, who lived in some old stables there, holding forth and foretelling doom and disaster to the wicked. He must have been the last of the "Ranters", from whom one house in that area gets its name. And there was a

Mr. May who built the three cottages at the top of Sandy Lane just below Ruffway, a house built for the curate by Mr. Gregory, the Vicar of Platt".

(My mother died in 1963 aged 96 years old.)

"REMINISCENCES" 1897-1980

Albert Bowen

I was born in one of the Forge Cottages, Wrotham Heath, 3rd of a large family in 1897. My first memory is of being in a pram during the Jubilee Celebrations held at the end of the Relief of Mafeking, in what is now Windmill Park, in those days called Maxwell's Park; until the 1960s this was an open space, used by the villagers of Platt and Wrotham Heath for recreation.

Forge Cottages were adjacent to the Forge, belonging to the Luxford family, father and son, farriers and blacksmiths – they shod the horses of men such as Mr. Whitburne of Addington, and of Captain Thomas of Wrotham Heath House, a pugnacious man who would invite others from the Royal Oak (then a small pub on the narrow main London to Maidstone road) to box on his lawn.

Colonel Bailey of Nepicar House owned land up to Askew Bridge, and the cricket ground was situated on what is now Nepicar Farm, the cricket team used to go to Milwood (home of the Lewis family) for tea.

My weekly pocket money was ½d spent on sweets, but deducted if I misbehaved. Mr. Percy Grace, later of Wrotham Heath House, started the local scout movement for Platt and District; gentry used pony traps for local travel and for reaching Borough Green Station. At Warren Wood, built for Dr. Charlewood Turner F.R.C.P., they kept goats and Mr. Baker, their gardener, took goats' milk and soup to any sick persons in Wrotham Heath. The Post Office at that time being situated where now is "The Rose Restaurant". I was a pupil at Platt Old School, and during the summer holidays of 6-7 weeks, the first two weeks were spent fruit picking and the last two weeks in the hop-fields. The money thus earned being kept for food and clothing for the family.

I also helped with work on the Golf Links, the Club House being converted from farm buildings with the granary at the rear, and play started around this time, Mr. Job being the first professional. I was at school till the age of 13, leaving to take up apprenticeship with Mr. F. G. Pierce.

At the age of 17 I ran away to join the West Kent Regiment on September 29th, 1914, going to France in January 1916 as Regimental Signalman with the seventh battalion of that regiment, at that time stationed near to the village of Bray in France, and was present during the Somme Offensive. Except for scratches and trench fever, I survived, serving in the Army until demobbed in April 1919; and was decorated with the Belgian Croix de Guerre for courage and devotion to duty during the last Flanders Offensive. I was a Founder Member of the British Legion.

France — March 1917   Albert Bowen

Albert Bowen (Seated)

My late wife, Hilda Ellen Lacey, the grand-daughter of Richard Lacey of Pond Cottage, Platt, had been a school-mate of mine. After some years we met again and decided to get married, so in November 1921 we became man and wife, the marriage taking place in the Church of St. Mary Platt.

At that time I was working for Mr. Pierce in his workshop situated at the bottom of Black Horse Lane, Borough Green, and I helped to build the first bus depot, the roof trusses of which were formed from hangers from an Aerodrome.

The Toll Gate, Wrotham Heath. Mr. and Mrs. Baldwin 1900

In order to find a home, Mr. Jack Gilbert of the "Brickmakers' Arms" converted the club-room of that pub into a dwelling for us. In 1940, owing to the general slump, I left the building trade and joined Shorts of Rochester, working on Sunderland Flying Boats, and later with the Medway Group, which was formed to work on bomb damage at Lewisham.

In 1947 we took over the "Black Horse Inn" at Borough Green, leaving there in 1953. After living in Norwood and Shirley, we finally returned to St. Mary Platt and settled in No.4 the Captain's Walk, where my dear wife died in April 1975.

PLATT COMMON

Kate Webb & Jack Terry

Some months ago, a most interesting piece appeared in "The Parish Pump", written by Olive Gilbert, where she mentioned the name of John Terry, who built "The Grange"; and we would like to enlarge on this.

Our Grandfather, Richard Terry, was a first cousin of the above named, and our family have lived on Platt Common for many years. Unfortunately we have no records that go further back than the early 1800's although we do have our Grandfather's Apprenticeship Indenture forms, dated 1855; whereby Richard Terry "is to be taught and instructed by a Mr. Bassett of Ightham, in the Trade, Art, Business and Mystery of a Boot and Shoemaker, in consideration of the sum of £20". According to this Indenture, it was to be paid in two instalments or moieties, from a fund known or called by the name of Doctor Layfield, the Trustees being Mr. John Bassett and a Mr. Thomas Spencer of Wrotham.

In the early 1800's Platt Common was just an open space, and proved to be the ideal location for a group of Irish smugglers, who settled in the area and claimed Squatter's Rights. Another branch of the Terry family lived at Terry's Lodge Farm, which is situated on the South side of the North Downs; this gave an excellent view of the main road to London and the village of Wrotham, thus giving the smugglers early warning of the advent of the Excise men in the area. The signalling system used by the smugglers is very interesting if only for its simplicity. The sheep and goats in a particular field on the farm were the key figures in this system – should it be "All Clear" for the Platt group to carry on with their operations the animals would be free and grazing as usual, but if the Excisemen were in the area, the sheep would be tethered in pairs by the farm group, thus warning their comrades on the Common to lie low and to keep their illicit Brandy out of sight till the danger had passed.

The site now occupied by "The Brickmaker's Arms" was reputed to be the meeting-place of the two groups whenever this was necessary. When the smugglers urgently needed to contact their Headquarters in Romney Marsh, a dog cart was despatched, piloted by a lightly built lad in order that the frail cart could carry the weight, and this must have had some connection with the foregoing. An old wooden ship's door made into a gate, with a beam across the top, was to be seen within living memory in the wall in Grange Road opposite the playing field, and on the beam were the words: "Accommodation for one able seaman". It would appear, according to the Indenture Papers, that by the middle of the Nineteenth Century, the smugglers had opted for a life of law and order.

Another interesting feature of the Common is the path at the top, which emerges in Grange Road just above "The Blue Anchor" - the correct name of this footpath is neither The Tin Path, nor Tin Pan Alley; but it is The Slype (pronounced Slip), which can be confirmed by study of the old ordnance maps. Those who are familiar with Rochester will know that the pathway between the Cathedral and the Castle, bears the same name, spelt in a similar manner. The unsightly remains of a corrugated fence on one side of our Slype is all that remains of a fence erected by John Terry of The Grange, which originally started from Grange Cottage, up the left hand side of Sandy Lane to prevent trespassing amongst his peacocks. At the top of this lane are May's Cottages, 1853, in one of which was once the home of Miss Day, the first County Librarian at Platt Memorial Hall, some 50 years ago.

Note: "Ruffway", facing the end of the lane was built for the Curate, the Reverend A.G. Phillips in 1897, and was later the home of Mr. and Mrs. Will Cadby, a talented couple, authors of children's books illustrated by Mr. Cadby's photographs taken in the adjacent woods. The 'actors' were local children, Mary Curtis, Queenie Higgins, Sadie Ladd and the Wilson family from the Thatched House. 'Finding a Fairy' and 'The Doll's Day' published by Mills & Boon at 2/- each in 1919.

PORTRAIT OF MY FATHER – HARRY FULLER 1869-1957
Belle Evans

Brushing out a hedgerow on a grey January morning, Mr. Harry Fuller paused for a moment: "I remember the time we used to work a 66 hour week for 1¼d per hour" he said. "The weekly pay was 6/3d in those days, or maybe, if you worked nights it would be 7/1; though if late starting, time was deducted and a weekly wage packet reduced."

"FARMING AT 87, 22 YEARS AFTER OFFICIAL RETIREMENT" – such were the headlines in the Kent Messenger, when my father was the Guest of Honour at a special supper-party given at the Memorial Hall in January 1957, when he was presented with 'This is your life'. Many friends were there to cheer and congratulate him, including a letter of congratulations from Lord Cornwallis. The occasion was kept a close secret from my father till the last moment, and all ended happily when he returned home to Porch Cottage, feeling very proud, but slightly confused.

Harry Fuller was born in Shipbourne, and when the family moved to the Chequers, Crouch, he walked daily to Platt (Old)

School, then under headmastership of Mr. Perkins. After leaving school he took on bird minding for his father James Fuller, who by that time had taken over Basted Farm, and Harry also did a period of service as house-boy to the Big House, and well remembered Walter (later Viscount) Monckton and his brother Lesley whom he taught to shoot – they were the grandsons of the founder of Basted Mill. As a lad on the farm, my father gained great knowledge of local wild life, which stood him in good stead later. In 1889 he married Lilian Dodd and lived in Bonhill, Crouch, subsequently moving to Porch Cottage, Platt, his home for the rest of his life. A remarkable man, forthright, punctual to the second, and a strict disciplinarian compared to present day standards.

In the early days our neighbours were Mr. and Mrs. Pearson and family, who kept the Post Office Stores, their daughter Clemmie helped with Sunday School, the Girls' Club, and other local activities. They worked long hours in the shop, as most goods such as rice, sugar, flour, etc. had to be weighed and put into paper-bags. There was also the Bakers (mentioned by Mrs. Dick Hollands in her memoirs) where lovely crusty loaves were available whenever wanted, the bread left over being made into bread-pudding at ½d per slice. This was much in demand, especially when the crowds of Londoners came to pick hops and fruit; they were paid in tin money which was changed at the shop for groceries, perhaps two pennyworth of bacon slices, or one pennyworth of broken biscuits to feed their large families.

Back view of Platt Vicarage (date unknown)

After a period of farming with his father, Harry became gamekeeper to Mr. Jim Smith of Basted House, and after the latter's death, as gardener to Mr. and Mrs. Alfred Collings, until retiring at 65. However, he was soon back at work, this time for Mr. Geoff Bacon, and there he stayed for another 22 years! "Might as well, die out of doors here, as at home," he would say, when asked why he carried on working, for he was an out-of-doors man, with never a grumble, regular as a clock, Harry Fuller lived his life amongst the fields he had always known. The animal he disliked being the fox, and his way of curing a ferret from biting was to put a hot pipe bowl on its nose: "They don't bite me after that," he said. On December 28th 1957 he died. Now times have changed, but memories linger on.

MEMORIES OF ST. MARY PLATT 1890 - 1982

Miss Elsie Revill

In the year 1890 my father – John Revill, purchased two plots of land in Platt, one of which contained the three cottages now known as 'Laurelcot', 'Littlecot' and 'Kelvin'. These were let at a rent of 2/6 each per week which included rates. The second plot of land was kept as a kitchen garden until Mr. Revill and family came to reside in Platt in 1909 occupying two of these cottages.

In the garden at the rear was a well into which a pail was lowered, by means of a rope, to a depth of some seventy feet, the only drinking water obtainable until the main supply was laid on. It may be interesting to note that the late Dr. Lipscombe of Wrotham took samples of this water from the well and found that it contained nearly as much iron as that from the Pantiles at Tunbridge Wells. It has been stated that the source of this spring is at Basted.

In 1907 it was decided to open a shop in the middle cottage now called 'Littlecot', and this meant removing the small window and replacing it by a shop-front. The present large window is exactly the same as in the past. The commodities sold ranged from a packet of pins to coal, the latter sold at 28lbs for 4½d and was fetched by customers with their own sacks. It was sold not later than 9.30a.m. in case the dust from the coal (kept in the cellar) should reach the shop floor. Apart from drapery the price list was as follows:-

Butter	– 6d or 8d per lb.
Margarine	– 4½d or 5d per lb
Bacon	– Back 8d per lb
Streaky	– 6d per lb.
Collar	– 5d per lb.
Sweets	– Boiled, 2ozs. for 1d, Assorted, 4oz. for 1d
Lard	– 5d or 6d per lb.
Sugar	– 2½d or 3½d per lb.
Biscuits	– 6d or 7d (special) per lb.
Sunlight Soap	– 2 tablets at 5d
Matches	– pkt of 12 boxes 3d or 4d
Cheese	– 5d, 6d or 10d per lb.

Every second or third Friday two pigs, killed by Mr. Hoppe, Butcher at Wrotham, were brought by him to be cut into joints for customers who collected their orders. Prices were: Loin – 8d per lb; streaky – 6½d per lb; collar – 7d per lb. Fresh produce for the shop was grown in the back garden.

In 1915 owing to the war it was found difficult to obtain stock so the shop was closed. As a side-line, however, my father had already acquired the meadow opposite the Brickmakers' Arms and he owned a horse and wagonette which he drove to convey anyone wishing to reach Borough Green Station, the fare being 1/- per person.

In closing the shop I still retain many memories of the kindness shown by customers who to the last helped to boost the sales and to support "the miniature Selfridges from London".

PLATT STORES & POST OFFICE & OTHER MEMORIES
Miss M.C. (Clemmie) Pearson
1896 - 1979

In May 1895 my father R.C. Pearson, came to Platt and
bought a small grocery business, now Platt Stores and Post Office. At
that time the floor only reached as far as the present step in the
centre of the shop, and from there, three or four steps led down to
the road.

Shortly after settling, he married, returning at once to his
shop, since being fruit and hop-picking time, the premises were
besieged by pickers from London, a tough lot in those days. In 1901
the shop was extended to the present size, and my father became
sub-Postmaster, opening a bake-house in the rear of the house, while
my mother started a drapery department.

We owned a horse and four-wheeler trap in which my father
drove the vicar, the Reverend G. Billing, on his parish visits, since
the latter was a cripple, and for many years he was a sidesman in
Platt Church, and sang in the choir. When the Reverend J.
Mallinson succeeded as Vicar, my father became the people's

Church Warden, and during this period he started the collection of photographs of previous Incumbents, which I understand now hang in the vestry.

In 1914 he joined "Dad's Army", and on losing the services of his baker, who joined up, my mother took over the bakery, and with the help of Daisy Stratton I attended in the shop.

Amongst many people doubtless remembered by older inhabitants of Platt were Mr. and Mrs. Will Cadby, authors of books for children illustrated by Mr. Cadby's photographs. There was Mr. Pyke to whom sick and ailing animals were taken for treatment and advice, Charlie Evans who drove his greengrocer's van to local villages and I believe as far as Tonbridge, Mr. Prentice who went out every evening whatever the weather to light the street lamps and to extinguish them each morning. He was sexton of the Church and his wife the cleaner there. I remember Mr. Pankhurst of Beechin Wood who held dances in the church-like barn opposite. Mr. Norman King-Smith of Platt Farm, subsequently owned by Richard Hearne (Mr. Pastry). Dales consisted of two cottages, in one of which lived the local cobbler Mr. Bill, my life-long friends, Cicely, Dolly and Tom Wolfe of "Potash". Henry Wilson who designed and lived in The Thatched House, a well-known artist and sculptor whose work may be seen in the Lady Chapel of the Church, a memorial to the Rev. G. Billing, and an ornamented cross in the churchyard. Of the four Wilson children, the only survivor is Pernel, known by her professional name of "Orea Pernel", a violinist, who gave me violin lessons. Yew Tree Farm was owned by Mr. and Mrs. Bradley, and on the death of her husband, Mrs. Bradley had "Threeways" built, selling Yew Tree to Captain Bertie Radcliffe, for whom the barn and farm house were converted into one dwelling by his friend Captain Austin Turner who had been a fellow prisoner of war in Germany during part of the First War.

I have been asked to say something of myself. After my father's severe illness, I had to leave school to help my mother, also assisting with the Infants' Sunday School, later taking a class of older children, and occasionally playing the organ for Sunday Services when the organist, Miss Palmer of St. Mary's Lodge, was away. Ada Baldock, Elsie Revill and I started a Girls' Club in the Memorial Hall and had some very happy evenings as Nellie Hollands and Sadie Ladd will remember.

My father lived in Platt for 50 years and died aged 72; my mother then sold the business and went to live in Borough Green, dying there aged 90. My three brothers have died and I am the only survivor of our family, but I return to Platt from Folkestone every year to visit old friends and the Reverend V. Kingston and Mrs. Kingston, whose parishioner I was during their Folkestone days.

PLATT STORES

(Continued by Olive Gilbert)

Having read Clemmie Pearson's memories of Platt Stores, I am reminded of her father's shop after it had been extended.

Platt Stores – R. C Pearson in apron.

On entering, loose stock such as sugar, currants and raisins, sweets etc., were sold at the counter on the left; and Mr. Pearson was adept at making cone-shaped bags from blue paper; the goods being weighed on brass scales, and poured into these bags with a little brass shovel. Overhead, on hooks attached to the ceiling (some of which still remain) were hung boy's and men's hob-nailed boots, together with dustpans, brushes, saucepans and such like. Ascending the step into the older part of the shop, was a counter on the left where grocery and goods which had to be cut were weighed, a special knife being used for cheese; customers were allowed to taste before purchasing. The centre was the Post Office and on the right, a counter supplying haberdashery, presided over by Mrs. Pearson. How well I remember going through the Blue Anchor passage (now closed) on my way to school, in order to gaze at that little window which displayed prettily trimmed hats with flowers and ribbons, made by Mrs. Pearson. It was indeed a wonderful shop where you could buy almost anything. I fear they have disappeared for ever, like the trimmed hats which I so admired, more than seventy years ago.

THE MINTERS OF STADDLESWOOD
Belle Evans

In 1901 two remarkable people came to Platt, Mr. and Mrs. Percy Minter, who stayed for a time with Mrs. Minter's brother, Frank West of Mill House, now Foxbury. Whilst there, they bought a piece of rough woodland, including an ancient oak tree, which has since unfortunately been felled. The house known as "Staddleswood" was built in 1903, and Mr. Percy Minter, and his wife, Mary, moved in.

Being a very talented person, Mrs. Minter soon had plans for the garden, and with the help of Mr. R. Prentice, Sexton of Platt Church these were put into operation. Lawns, flower borders, and some woodland full of wild flowers made a most attractive setting. Almost immediately the Minters became active members of the village, always delighted to have plays performed in their garden, fetes took place, and the tennis court was used by many, including the Men's Club and the Girl's Club, with weekly Bowls matches played against other local teams.

Indeed Mrs. Minter's life was a full and busy one – she supervised the Band of Hope, the Primrose League for the Young, conducted the W.I. Singing Circle, and for many years trained the Church Choir, taught in the Sunday School and edited the Parish Magazine up to her death at the age of 92 in 1933. On October 3rd 1937, the choir stalls were dedicated to her memory, whilst the pulpit was given by the Rev. Arthur Cross in memory of his mother, and dedicated at the same service.

Platt Mill, 1912.

Mr. Minter worked for the Admiralty from 1886-1926 as Director of Contracts for the Navy, and was awarded the C.B.E. for his services during the first World War. During the 52 years he lived in Platt, he was Churchwarden for 40 years, treasurer of the

Parochial Church Council, a manager of Platt Primary School, and was singing in the choir within a few months of his death. He was a Founder Member of Wrotham Heath Golf Club, and its treasurer for many years – the game remained his chief hobby, winning a silver spoon at the age of 80! After retiring from the Admiralty, 'Mr. Percy' bought Cloggatts Farm which included a large field now known as King George's Field, which he left for a small sum to the local Cricket and Football clubs, wishing it to be used by the inhabitants of Platt.

At his death in 1955 the first chapter of the history of "Staddleswood" ended, and after living with the Minters for 41 years, I can say that they were the most loving and devoted couple one could ever wish to see, despite the great disparity in their respective ages. My husband Horace and I then moved into Fir Tree Cottage, where on the front wall we were surprised to find an Ordnance Bench Mark which shows that at this point the height of the land above sea-level has been measured and recorded on ordnance survey maps, indicating that we are 329 feet above sea-level. The name is thought to come from the piece of metal which is inserted in the horizontal incision as a "bench" or support for the surveyor's levelling rod. The "arrow" is the official Government Survey Mark.

"THOSE WERE THE DAYS"

Stanley Box

I was born on December 24th 1904 at Mill Cottages, Platt, where my brother and his wife now live. The mill was then owned by Mr. Frank West for whom my father worked. At that time the machinery was driven by a steam-engine, hence the tall chimney which dominated the sky-line; the boiler-room with its domed ceiling I think is still there. The Mill was then four storeys high and behind was a well which was twice as deep as the mill was high, this supplied the water for the driving force required. As the cottages had no piped water, we had to collect this in buckets etc. Later the steam engine was replaced by a huge gas-driven engine, the thump, thump, thump from this could be heard over most of Platt. Before the Memorial Hall was built there was a pond on that site, and what is now "Micawbers" was a store for Platt Mill. On the Eastern end there is still a pulley which was used to hoist sacks of corn to the door beside it, this had a chain which was harnessed to a horse which my father walked across the road to where the Hall now stands, this raised the sacks weighing 21 cwts. from the ground to the door and was then emptied into storage bins.

I was most interested in the articles by Johnnie Geddes when he described the dairy at Great Comp, and I too remember collecting milk and cream from there with other children walking at 6.30a.m. rain or shine, winter or summer, seven days a week delivering in Platt. Mine was to a Doctor Caersor at Stone Ridge, for which I received 1/6 per week. I also remember the Coronation party, in celebration of George V's accession, which was held in "Maxwell's Park" (now Windmill Park). Each of us had a Coronation mug, and water for making tea was boiled in a traction-engine belonging to Luke Terry.

I was in the Church choir for several years, and how we looked forward to the choir outings, which usually meant a day at the sea-side. On Saturday evenings we went to a Boy's Guild, run by Mr. King-Smith in a hut at Platt Farm. About this time, four local boys were singing "I'm forever blowing bubbles" whilst on their way home from Wrotham, they were caught by a policeman called Pussyfoot and each boy fined 5/- "for disturbing the peace"! How different things are today!

I left school in 1918 and went to work in Platt Mill, which at that time operated a twelve hour shift, alternate weeks. I therefore worked from 6a.m. to 6p.m. (Saturdays 6a.m. - 4p.m.) or from 6p.m. to 6a.m. at 10/- per week. Later, for twenty-seven years I drove a taxi for Mr. Kennett, and had many interesting journeys, during which time I saw most members of the Royal Family. One day I was waiting for a client outside St. Margaret's, Westminster, where a "Person of Note" was being married, one amongst the crowd of onlookers had quite a chat with me, and after he left I was informed that he was John Wayne, the film star. For a short time during the last war "The Studios" adjacent to "The Thatched House" were occupied by Peter Townsend (then Equerry to the late king) – a brave man that he was, I well remember his coming to collect his belongings when the Court moved to Windsor. It was during the Doodle-bug period, and he was scared stiff, asking for a lift to avoid London. In those days one knew everybody in Platt, how different it is today!

MEMORIES OF WROTHAM HEATH GOLF CLUB
Nancy Box

It was in 1906 that my late father, L.C. Job began making the nine hole golf course at Comp, later to be known as the Wrotham Heath Golf Club. When some of the fairways were being made, Roman coins and pottery were found, and they were taken to the British Museum. The land belonged to the Leybourne Parish, a clause in the deeds stated that no golf should be played on Good Fridays, and that a room be reserved in the Club House for religious services, should this be needed, to replace the chapel at Comp Corner which had been demolished. The club house was originally an oast house, and my father who had been appointed professional and greenkeeper used one of [the] kilns for his work-shop, but later they were made into dressing-rooms, a lounge and a bar installed, with locker room and dining room upstairs, and a comfortable home joining on for us. I was the eldest of the family, and we all went to Platt school walking to and fro each day. My brother and I were in Platt Church choir, so that with choir practice and going to church on Sundays, we did a lot of walking in those days.

The first World War came, and my father joined the army and was sent out to France, the club house was taken over by the army and soldiers were billeted there until huts were made for them on the links. Two guns were erected about two hundred yards from our house, and a search light on the highest point, it was very exciting watching the searchlights trying to find the German planes, but very frightening when the guns started firing. I remember a balloon coming down on the course, and one in Mr. Heron-Maxwell's field, Mrs. Heron-Maxwell taking refreshments out to the men who landed safely from it.

The war over, my father safely home, so golf started again. I finished school and was employed by the club to help my mother with the catering, four-course lunches at 2/6 and teas 1/-. My aunt, Miss Brooker, was training to become a nurse, but her doctor advised her to get an out-door job, so she came to live with us, and worked on the course for many years. My father was very keen on the putting side of golf and eventually became the champion putter. I was on the course playing whenever I had the chance, and with a handicap of eight, decided to enter for the Girls Open Championship. Three cards had to be sent in, signed by three different members of the club, and it was a great thrill to hear that I was one of twenty-three girls who had qualified to play, but my hopes of winning were dashed in the first round as I was beaten by a French girl with a handicap of one. Many notable people came to the club but our greatest surprise came one day when we heard from

Mereworth Castle that they were bringing the Prince of Wales, later the Duke of Windsor, over for a game of golf. I felt very proud that day and I handed him the pen to write his name in the visitors' book.

My sisters and I had always been keen on acting, so with friends from the village, we started a concert party. Miss Bright the Headmistress at Platt School taught me to play the piano, and Miss Turner who lived at Warren Wood helped us with our sketches. There was a Mission room at the bottom of Windmill Hill where two detached houses now stand, we gave concerts there, and at Platt Memorial Hall, and once took a party to Gravesend. The star of our show was Mrs. Kate Dixon who still lives in Wrotham Heath, she always brought the house down singing "Don't Dilly Dally on the Way". She entered a talent competition at the Granada, Maidstone, and won it singing that song.

The second war was just starting when Stan and I were married at Platt Church. We were lucky to start our married life in this bungalow at Ford Lane where we still live, near the club, so that we were able to carry on playing golf, but in 1940 German planes started to visit us, bombs were dropped on the course, on Mr. Pierce's farm opposite, and in the woods and fields around about. A German airman was found hanging by his parachute in a tree by the fourth tee, and a Polish airman landed his plane on the course. I happened to be there when the plane came to a stop, so was able to help him, and as he was only shaken, we made for the club house where he was given refreshments. Captain Turner, our chief warden, was sent for, army personnel came out and soldiers were sent out to guard the plane, and as the airman could not speak English, it was late when final particulars were taken, so that my father did not pay his usual visit to Wrotham Heath that night. What a blessing that was, as The Royal Oak had a direct hit and there were many casualties. We often look back and wonder how we survived it all, but we did, and when it was all over a friend of ours bought one of the army huts and made it into a comfortable home. She had a shock one day when a golfer drove his ball through one of her windows and it landed in a rice pudding that was standing on her kitchen table; so although we do not play these days, but just watch the game on television, Wrotham Heath Golf Club will always hold many happy memories for both of us.

THOMAS PASCALL AND THE BRICKFIELDS

F. G. Bennett

In 1898 the Brickfields at Platt (now the site of Platt Industrial Estate) were taken over from Captain Walmersley by Thomas Pascall. This property provided the best moulding sand for brick-making.

Fred and George Bennett were very skilled men who did all the burning, setting, loading and unloading of the kilns. A brick kiln would contain around 140,000 bricks, using about 24 tons of coal for the burning process – this took some 3 days and nights, and a cooling period of 4 days. All the bricks for extensions to Harrow School, and the fireplace brickettes for Sandringham House, both orders were burnt to a special colour – clay and loam was obtained from the site of the Brickfields with which moulding was all done by hand. There were 4 varieties of sand: black sand, building sand, silver sand for glass blowing, coarse and moulding sand. Thomas Pascall made great improvements and introduced the first hanging Nib tiles; he sometimes drove the steam engine railway himself, which operated the clay mills as well as handling the trucks.

London refuse came by rail to a siding alongside called "Spencer's Siding" in order to fill in the cavities left by the removal of loam and sand. The empty trucks were then reloaded with bricks and tiles. Refuse was dirty smelly stuff, chiefly waste from London hotels, but "dirty" money was paid. The findings were good, articles of gold and silver and other precious objects were found in this refuse and rag and bone dealers would come and buy, and with the money, the big stone beer bottles were replenished from "The Brickmaker's Arms", much needed refreshment by thirsty men working in the hot and exhausting craft of brick and tile making.

In 1914 at the outbreak of the First War, production had to stop, though George Bennett carried on to get all contents of the Kiln burnt and removed, and he was the last man to leave the yard. In 1920 things got going again, but the first big Kiln was burnt by amateurs, burnt to a clinker, and consequently a dead loss; however, George Bennett returned and supervised until he passed on in 1926.

The General Strike, with coal unobtainable, the yard was temporarily crippled again. Then in 1925 Black Sand was used in moulding, and when burnt gave the tiles and bricks a fantastic Rustic finish, hence the 2 inch Brick and rustic Tile were in great demand. Whole contents of kilns were purchased by a Government Department and used to build Post Offices, Telegraph Exchanges, Hospitals and other public buildings in Maidstone, Hastings, Portsmouth, naming but a few. About 36 men were employed, most work was piece-work at good wages, 7 Brickmakers, 12 Tile Moulders, Burners, Crowders and Grinders, all very skilled men in the making of moulds for Arch Bricks, Copings, Specials and Ornamentals, with knowledge of shrinking and burning of wet clay to give finish to the article in hand.

Mr. Albert Bowen was the Mould Specialist for many years and in 1935 when Tile Moulders were digging their clay, some 9ft below field surface, a collection of charred embers of wood, some clay vessels and bones were found which Archaeologists identified as Roman remains.

In 1939 the Yard was closed again until after the Second War ended. Many good and experienced Moulders did not return; Bottom Yard lease and materials were running out; Hop Kilns in Kent had suffered from bomb damage and no tiles could be found for repairs. So Albert Bowen made a special Mould and I made 34,000 Hop Kiln Tiles from it, which were purchased by Wallace, Builders of Maidstone, whose firm bought the lot to ensure that Kent got them. In 1948 we saw the last year of production, and by 1950 everything was cleared and everyone had left, with the exception of Mr. Henry Knipe.

Thomas Pascall was Chairman of Platt Parish Council, and a Magistrate on the Bench at West Malling. His only son was killed in the First World War.

"POTTERS, POTS, BRICKS AND TILES"

F. G. Bennett

Harry and Henry Knipe, father and son, were the last of five generations of family potters, and before the First War they lived in Platt. They were employed by Thomas Pascall in the local Brickyards (see June issue of "Platt News") but moved to Gravesend in 1914; Harry with his skills to Vickers, Henry enlisted in the R.A.F.

In 1920 they both returned to Platt Brickfields Top Yard, Harry to pottery, while Henry took over the foreman's job of bricks and tiles. Harry was a master of the potter's wheel, using a flint as a bearing or pivot for the wheel, operated by foot treadle which gave perfection and smoothness. He had exceptionally long arms and fingers, although when making a batch of chimney pots, he needed assistance to turn the heavy geared wheel, which was turned by hand, to make 24" to 36" pots, using 120lbs of clay for one big pot alone, one arm inside, and one arm outside to float them up on the wheel, – all pot clay was double ground to ensure smoothness. In order to save space in the kiln, chimney pots were filled with flower pots, and many a garden basket or money box was the gift of Harry Knipe to Brickfield workers, if and only if one admired his work. He was tutor in the craft of a potter to the late Mrs. Heron-Maxwell of Great Comp.

At the close of the Yards in 1950, Henry Knipe's job as foreman came to an end, and the sale of the Top Yard to Portland Cement Company enabled him to return to pottery. Thanks to the latter company, he had the use of the engine and clay mills, and access to surplus weathered clay, to end his days as a master of the craft of a potter.

I had helped him to grind his clay and with the burning of the old pot kiln, this proved much too big and costly, so he cut the burning hours, but found his pots were coming out under burnt. Then he built a smaller kiln in the old drying shed, thereby getting better results with his ornamental pottery and giving him a quicker turn-over. Some London firms were keen to buy and sell at treble the price he charged, but age was beginning to tell on him, so he visited Aylesford Priory and made good friends with Italian potters from Rome and tried their modern pottery wheels, which made smaller objects. The Priory potters visited Henry at Platt, and realised what a good potter he was; they tried hard to persuade him to end his days at the Priory, but his sister prevented him. So he carried on here, and on a good day could make 1,000 flower pots, though he never conquered the art of glazing, for he could not afford white china clay.

When he died, much of his work was smashed by vandals, the last to be made by the fifth generation of family potters.

Henry Knipe, Potter

Apart from his craft he was a knowledgeable and erudite man, a great reader with special interest in Ancient Greece, and he could recite passages from Shakespeare by heart, discussing the books he borrowed from the local County Library. He could never pronounce his R's so it would be "wough weather", - and an amusing incident occurred when the morning goods train put off a truck of unusual contents: commenting to the Guvnor "Twuck of dung, twuck of

dung, what do we want with a twuck of dung for in the Brickfields?"
– "For my blasted asparagus bed, of course," was the Governor's
reply.

After Henry Knipe's death I was asked by Mrs. Esme Walford
MBE to dismantle the old table and wheel in order that a place for
them could be found in Maidstone Museum. The primitive cottage
where he and his sister lived has been demolished; the Brickfields
and Yards are now the site of Calor Engineering Company, and
Platt Industrial Estate.

THE BRICKYARDS

Olive Gilbert

One day this last Summer, I wandered up to the brickyard
(now called Platt Industrial Estate) and my mind went back to my
childhood, and I thought how different it all is now. In the past the
kiln fires were burning brightly and you could wander where you
wished. These brickyards were in two sections, known as the bottom
yard, where the brick kilns were, and the top yard, where the pottery
kiln and the other tile kilns were situated. A skilled potter, Henry
Knipe worked on his own further up, until vandals destroyed all his
stock. In the top yard was a big pond, where children fished with
jam jars, and you could walk along to the little ponds where tadpoles
were to be found. Primroses and violets in the Spring, sometimes the
wild orchid – now it is enclosed in a chain-link fence with "Keep
Out" notices.

One of my earliest recollections is being taken by my father,
who was Manager of the Brickyards, to the office on a Sunday
morning to collect the post, while I was sat there on a high stool.
Just outside the office was the big bell that stood on a jutting sand

rock (now flattened and planted with shrubs). This bell was rung to call the men to work at 6a.m., again at 12 o'clock for dinner, 1p.m. to start the afternoon's shift, and finally at 5.30p.m. the end of their working day. I also remember going with my father to visit the burners on a Sunday morning near Christmas time, when the gate at the entrance to the brickyards was shut once a year, as it was a Private Road, through a public footpath which led to Wrotham, a pleasant walk through the fields beyond.

There was also a little engine that came from the top yard to the railway siding (some rusty rails were still visible until recently) to fetch the trucks left by the luggage train up in to the yards, taking them down again loaded with bricks, tiles, sand, etc., and bringing up the coal.

The place where the warehouses and small factories are now situated, was a field where mushrooms abounded, and we would get up very early in the morning to gather them and have them stewed in milk for breakfast. I remember when the big pond at the entrance to the Wrotham fields was hired by Wrotham School, and a cradle was built for swimming lessons, and many boys from Platt joined them.

Then there was the annual Flower Show, held in the field opposite "The Brickmaker's Arms", quite an event. Two large marquees were erected along-side the railway, one for flowers and fruit and for vegetables, one for live-stock and so on. All sorts of cookery were shown, including roasted potatoes. "Pettigrove's" a well-known travelling amusement show arrived with round-a-bouts, switch-backs, swings and helter-skelter and other things of amusement, plus a brass band from West Malling, which played for dancing in a corner of the field in the evening.

When the First War started, the kilns had to be blacked out, which was a sad blow to everyone.

"73 YEARS IN PLATT"

Ivy King (late Bennett)

In 1902 when I was one year and ten months old, and my sister Olive had not long been born, my parents, George and Rose Bennett moved from Borough Green to No.2 Fir Tree Cottages, Platt, where previously my uncle Fred Bennett and his wife Hester had lived until they moved to the house now called "Grottan", formerly Sandpits Cottage in Grange Road. My mother told me that they kept a pony in a lean-to shed at the end of their house. Our neighbours next door were an elderly couple called Hodder – Mr. Hodder had a long white beard and moustache, and his wife always wore a black lace, or a beaded bonnet.

At that time there were no other houses on our side of the road to Borough Green, till one came to Black Horse Lane, with the exception of a large black barn, and a slaughter house, once a stable and now a private dwelling, on the land occupied by the Norman Estate. Nor were there any houses up in the woods where Staddleswood and Bracken Hill now stand, so my Aunt kept pigs and chickens, letting them roam over a large area where there were wells. At one time, we were threatened with eviction by the landlord, but Staddleswood had been built by then, and owned by Mr. and Mrs. Percy Minter, so they bought these cottages and I lived in No.2 till 1973.

I remember Bracken Hill being built, and seeing the driveway made, and the fence which was a boundary between us, over which rambler roses were trained; when in full bloom these were a well-known sight. Trees and shrubs were planted and the Bird-Cherry in still there. In those days since the traffic was horse drawn, we could play on the road, hop-scotch, and spin our tops, and we girls would trundle our wooden hoops, and the boys their iron ones. They used a home-made wheel-barrow in which to collect the horse manure for their fathers' gardens. Sometimes the Hunt went by and (as Olive Gilbert has already mentioned in last May's issue of "Platt News") gates had to be kept closed when cattle were driven to market.

I well remember the day of mourning for King Edward VII when my father took my sister and I to the Memorial Service in Platt Church; we wore white dresses with black sashes and white straw hats trimmed with black ribbon. In those days when anyone died in the village, the Sexton would toll the Church bell and one of the Alms House ladies was called to lay out the dead, for which she was paid, though a drop of brandy was needed as well!

When I was twelve years old I went to work for Mr. and Mrs. Will Cadby who lived at Ruffway, Platt Common, and I had to get up very early in the morning in order to take a big milk can to Great Comp dairy, sometimes returning with fresh butter as well. After being given breakfast at the Cadby's I had to help in their house till 8.30am, by which time it was a rush on foot to be at Borough Green Council School by 9 a.m. In the afternoon I returned to Ruffway to help and to collect letters for posting, a daily job and all day Saturday, for which I was paid 1/6 per week, but I loved the Cadby's and my work there, till September 1914. I then went to Staddleswood to be trained as house-parlour maid. Whilst there, I accompanied Mrs. Minter who was choir mistress, to choir practice in the Church, carrying a bag containing hymn books, and whilst she played the organ I worked the organ pump. I also had to take brass and cleaning materials, in order to polish the right-hand side of the Communion rails; the left-hand side polished by a servant of Mr. Lewis, the Lay Reader, who lived at Millwood, Wrotham Heath. In those days during Church services, the boys sat behind the font, and girls in the back pew on the other side of the aisle.

During the First World War, Stone Cottage (until recently owned by the late Brigadier Keane) was occupied by nuns, and we could see a big Cross hanging in the attic, and we heard organ music and chanting. My father did odd jobs for them, a list of which was placed in a box outside their door where he would find payment. One of the nuns kept a bag of sweets for my sister hidden in the folds of her habit, and another was said to be a German spy! During that war, we saw many troops and cavalry and guns going past on their way to a Channel port en route for France, sometimes they stopped and asked for water, but the only food we could spare were apples. My brother, Tom, truly a son of Platt, was amongst the first to join up in August 1914, and was in the Army throughout the war, winning the M. M. and Bar, for gallantry under heavy shell fire in the Battle of the Somme. He was chosen to lay the first wreath of poppies when the plaque, in memory of those in Platt who were killed in action, was unveiled outside the Memorial Hall, as described by Mrs. Nora Collings in "Platt News" of January 1979.

I remember the Women's Institute being started in 1920 in the Old Schools, where entertainment was provided by local talent, Mrs. Alf Fawcett as pianist, Mrs. Murphy played the cello and Mrs. Pyke sang "Cockles and Mussels, alive, alive O!" and other soloists. That is where I first learnt to dance, and I joined the first outing to the sea-side, when we were driven in one of the Mill lorries, sitting on forms and chairs, covered by a green canvas top, since there were no coaches in those days. My grandmother was Mary Anne Terry, sister of Squire John Terry of The Grange, to whom the three stained glass windows on the South wall of Platt Church are dedicated. My father planted the first beech hedge in the drive-way opposite the South porch and looked after the graves. My parents are buried in the Churchyard, next to other members of the Bennett family.

A MAN OF KENT

1895-1983

F. G. Pierce

When I married Miss Agnes Fife in 1924, two Kentish farming families of long-standing were surely united, since my mother's maiden name was Woodger, a family which can be traced to Charles and Isabella Woodger (1684-1754). They lived and farmed at Aldon, recorded in Addington Church:

"Francis Tresse (grandfather of Isabella) was a Church Warden at Mereworth, and died in 1704 – a Freeholder he left one messuage, one orchard, and four parcels of land, being 15 acres at Alderne, to the wife of Charles Woodger, and her heirs." The Woodgers farmed and lived at Comp, possibly from 1792-1880, meanwhile my grandfather Pierce had been hop-farming at Marden until capital ran out, so things were not easy for him. This was the reason why my father William T. Pierce came to Comp in 1890 where there were no hops, instead produce for Covent Garden was cultivated and taken to Borough Green station by horse and cart. Casual labour was employed, both men and women, many of whom would take short cuts on foot to the farm from Wrotham Heath, Offham, Platt and even further afield, which accounts for many of the local footpaths still in use. In those early days, cattle drovers took their herds on foot to Maidstone market once a month, a tricky job when animals strayed into private properties! This however was before I was born in 1895.

The Pierce Family

I lost my mother when I was eight years old, leaving my father with four young children, of whom I was the second. Later he married a Miss Perkins, whose father was school-master at Platt Old School, and where Miss Perkins was a teacher.

We lived in the old farmhouse at Comp Corner until 1911, when we moved to Highlands Farm. After two years at Platt School we went to Mereworth, a good school at that time, so for three years my older brother and I walked 2½ miles to school and back each day, till my father bought us two ancient bicycles, and well I remember cycling down Beech Hill with no brakes working!

On leaving school my heart was in farming and working on the farm with my father, which I did till the 1914 war started. Being of farming stock I naturally wanted to join an Artillery or Cavalry Regiment, but as no further recruits were wanted at Chatham in those regiments, it was suggested that with my experience of horses I should join the Royal Engineers. This I did as a carpenter, and was given as a test job, to make a dove-tailed box, the one thing I had learnt to make at school in wood-work classes. As I was used to fencing and making gates with 6 inch nails, this was an advantage with the REs when the construction or demolition of pontoon bridges were needed at any time.

I was sent to France in June 1915, and was lucky enough to suffer only minor scratches during the remainder of the war, whereas my brother William, who was called up during the last months of the war, went to France and was mortally wounded; such is the irony of Fate. It was during a scattered march behind the front line on the eve of the Battle of the Somme, while in readiness to construct a pontoon bridge, that I happened to meet a friend from

Platt, this was Albert Bowen (West Kent Regiment) who still remembers this brief encounter; we were indeed "all in it together".

When I returned from France at the end of the war, I agreed with my father that we should develop fruit growing, and we gained much good advice from East Malling Research Station, and were encouraged to intensify our cultivation to produce more food, by growing corn and potatoes etc., which were driven to Borough Green station for despatch to Covent Garden. I also wanted to start pig-breeding since we could use them as a means of orchard grazing where at this time they were running under cobnut trees, impossible to use horses or any type of cultivator under such low trees. As time went on the cost of growing cobnuts became uneconomic, so the pigs were transferred to open yards and farm buildings.

During the Second War bombs were dropped from a German plane during an air-raid on Comp Farm and on Highlands Farm, one bomb narrowly missing the pig-house containing some 100 pigs! Some of the enemy crew landed on our farm, one in an apple tree. Now we keep some 1500 pigs with less labour involved. During this last war I did Home Guard duty at Offham, and was asked to join the Agricultural Surveying Team, to see that all farm land was being fully used for maximum production, and I had five parishes under my supervision. Now we have more modern varieties of fruit on smaller trees, and with more up-to-date equipment and machinery a bigger unit is more viable. My father (who died in 1949) always said:

"Young men, young horses and young hops make a farm successful."
Today I would say: "Good men, modern machinery and modern
varieties of trees will make a business prosper." Now my two sons are
married and successfully running the whole business. My three
daughters have all married farmers, and I am glad to say are not
living far away. My wife died in 1973, the greatest sadness of my life,
but I am the lucky Grandad of seventeen grandchildren, and one
great grandchild, all of whom are well and healthy. I am now retired
and live at Hillcrest.

MRS. KATE DIXON
3 DAISY COTTAGES, WROTHAM HEATH

I was born within the sounds of the anvil, one of seven children of Alfred Broad and his wife Alice, our home being a Forge Cottage in Wrotham Heath when Mr. Luxford and his son Fred were blacksmiths to whom local landowners and farmers brought their horses to be shod, Colonel Whitburne's race horses, lovely creatures they were, and many others.

When it was safe from the heat of the forge, we sat on the wall which separated it from our house and watched the horses being shod and horse shoes made, a nice warm place in Winter. My father (whose parents lived up Windmill Hill) worked on the railway at 19/- per week and that was hard work. The rails were laid by hand, no machines in those days, but his job ended in 1918 when, in the fog, a troop train killed a fellow worker, and my father was so shocked that it turned his brain. He was a lot of trouble to my mother and us girls, our brothers being away at the war.

When I was young, I used to go hop-picking with my mother, and with the money earned she bought us new clothes for winter. A special train ran from London to Borough Green, bringing the East Enders, a wagon collected the heavy boxes and some of the smaller children; you could walk on the roads in those days of horse traffic, so the pickers wheeled their belongings in old prams, hand-carts, anything on wheels, to the huts on a farm near Offham. The huts were not very nice, very small, and the pickers were allowed one bundle of faggots per day for cooking and making tea. You picked the hops into a bin, a strong heavy wooden structure lined with fine strong mesh, into which the hops were put. A Bin man looked after you and your 10-12 bins, a chap to measure your pickings which would then go into a large bag called a poke; a wagon collected these pokes which were driven to the kilns to be dried and bagged again into very large tall bags, packed very tight, ready for the Hop Market. The Dryers were picked men who knew what to do and who worked all night keeping the charcoal fires burning. 1/- was paid for 8 or 9 bushels. It was hard work, but the Londoners enjoyed the country and if fine they would sing all day, it was lovely to hear them and the children could have lots of fresh fruit. I think it was one of the things which have gone for good. It was part of our lives and we made good friends. A sample of hops from the Oast House, put into a flannel bag and warmed, will help tooth- or ear-ache, and if put under a pillow will help one to sleep. We also went to pick fruit for Mrs. Pierce, (step-mother of Mr. Fred Pierce) she was a good woman, very nice and kind.

I remember Mr. and Mrs. John Baker who worked for Mrs. Turner, widow of Dr. Francis Charlewood Turner of Warren Wood, she was a dear lady, loved by everyone, she ran Mother's Meetings in the Mission Room, and her family joined in the village 'Do's', and always found costumes needed for theatricals. When she died her grave was lined with flowers. Mr. and Mrs. Frank Baker worked for the Miss Mansells of Nepicar Lodge, but these ladies were not very well received by the village folk, since they wired off the Deals which was our playground, but of course they mostly lived in Wales. I remember Miss du Boot of Huntsman's Lodge. The Hunt met outside the Royal Oak, a small pub in those days, and when my father was a young man and a great pal with the hounds, he would give a display in the meadow opposite calling each hound by name. He was given a jockey's cap of many colours and a whip and nicknamed "Pretty Cap", a name which went with him to the end of his life. The Kennels were opposite Ford Place and are now converted into a bungalow. I also remember the Miss Gregories, daughters of a former Vicar, and his successor the Rev. George Billing, who was crippled with arthritis, He gave food to school children from Crouch; people were very poor in those days.

We went to school at Platt National School, trespassing through Platt Woods which were private, so we had to avoid meeting the keeper, Mr. Crouch known as "Crongy", and on our way home we would call at 'Nanny' Bird's cottage (now called Lime Tree Cottage) for a drink of water, knowing we should be given a little something to eat. George Bird and his wife were well-liked, as were Mr. and Mrs. Harrington who lived near the windmill, and I remember when it was burnt down.

I live in No.3 Daisy Cottages, named after a daughter of Thomas Styles, Innkeeper of The Royal Oak in 1882. There in a conveyance dated 1844 "In fee of Half an Acres of Land near the Royal Oak Inn, in the Parish of Wrotham in Kent, between Henry

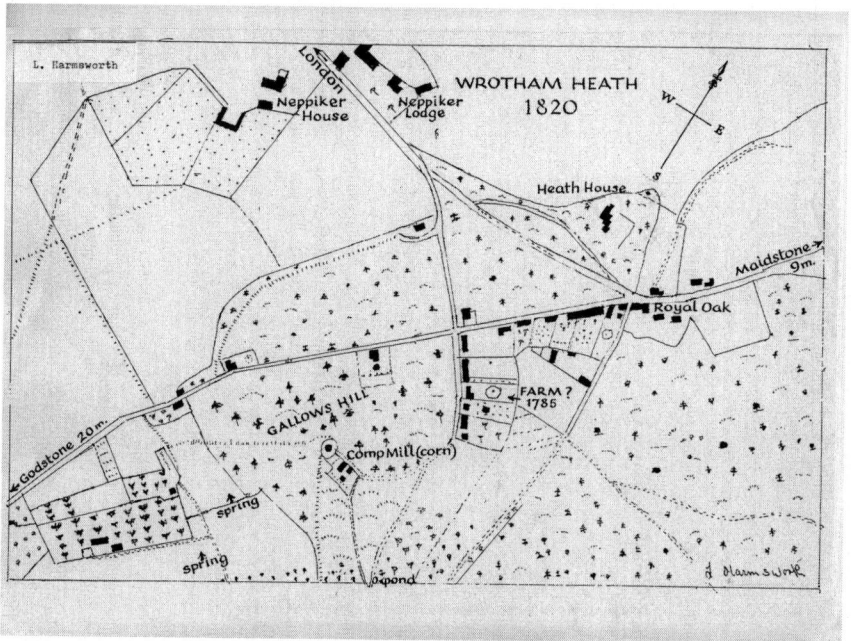

Hughes Esq and Messrs James and John Underwood". Another Conveyance dated 1865 "For four Messuages or Tenements and Hereditments at Wrotham Heath in the Parish of Wrotham

between John and James Usherwood and Mr. Stephen Constable". I remember Mr. Pollicot, Manager of the Royal Oak, we played in his garden with his girls. The pub was sold for £360 in 1903 to Mr. Findlay who was succeeded by Mr. John Swift in 1912, a well-liked man, who would help anyone and was sadly missed when he left. His daughter Vi (now Mrs. Treadgold) is still with us, as is Nancy (now Mrs. Stanley Box), whose parents managed the Golf Club House. She got up concerts, played the piano and produced plays, both in the Mission Room and later in the Memorial Hall. In those days we were like one big family and very happy together.

WROTHAM HEATH

Violet Treadgold

The original "Royal Oak" at Wrotham Heath was built about 1760, as a licensed Ale House, though no doubt there had been a Posting House for stage coaches, being on the London to Dover road. The Inn took its name from the war ship, and not from the neighbouring tree, which was a sycamore, and Stanley Box remembers as a boy, the iron rings fixed to the trunk to which travellers could tether their horses. From documents in the Archives Department in County Hall, Maidstone, it has been impossible to trace the first landlord, but in 1787:

"Samuel Sheafs of the Parish of Wrotham, acknowledges to owe to our Sovreign Lord and King, the sum of £10 to be levied on several Goods, Chattels, Land and Tenements, by way of Recognizance to his Majesty's use. Upon condition that if the said Samuel Sheafs who is this day licensed to keep a common Ale House or Victualling House at the sign of The Royal Oak with the said Parish or House where he dwells for the term of one year only, from the 29th day of September, 1787 shall keep good Order and Government, and suffer no disorder to be committed, or unlawful Games to be used in the said House,

Yard, Garden or Backfide (?) thereunto belonging, during the continuance of the said Licence. Then this Recognizance to be void or else to remain in full force".

Signed September 3rd 1787.

Subsequent landlords were: Thomas Kern 1839
William Hollands 1847
Thomas Edward Usher 1855
Thomas Styles 1882 (Manager Pollicot)
G. Findlay 1903-12.

THE ROYAL OAK, WROTHAM HEATH.

In that year my father John Swift became the landlord, and in a photograph of that date, a horse-drawn farm wagon and a waggonette with coachman are shown, together with the tariff charges. (Bearing in mind the value of £1 at that time, and that the average wage for a farm labourer was 16/- per week.)

On the London Maidstone Road, 25 miles from London.

THE ROYAL OAK,
Wrotham Heath. *1912*

:: TARIFF ::

BREAKFAST
Plain.. 9d.
With Eggs or Meat ....1s. 3d.

LUNCH OR SUPPER
Cold Meat, Pickles, Salad
    and Cheese ....1s. 6d.
Hot Joint, Vegetables,
    Sweets and Cheese ....2s. 6d.

TEA
Plain.. 9d.
With Eggs or Meat ....1s. 3d.

Late Dinner by arrangement.
Bedroom, single 1s. 6d., double 3s. 0d.
Use of Bathroom with h. & c. extra.

EXCELLENT ACCOMMODATION FOR
    . . . MOTORISTS AND CYCLISTS.
PARTIES CATERED FOR.

ACCOMMODATION FOR CARRIAGES
MOTORS and CYCLES.

G. FINDLAY, *Proprietor.*

To Be Returned to Mr Swift. 9d. Wrotham Heath.

There was a stable opposite The Royal Oak which my father moved back into the fields to serve as a cow shed when the London-Maidstone road was widened in 1925. Another photograph shows that presumably the owners of the Inn were Jude Hanbury and Co. of Canterbury, succeeded by Leney's of Wateringbury. Here I spent my childhood, often watching the horses being shod in the nearby forge – (see "Reminiscences" by Albert Bowen, August 1977 of The

Parish Pump – now called Platt News). At the age of 15 I was apprenticed to a hair-dressing establishment at Swanley, subsequently taking an "Improver" course in Maidstone, and when fully qualified I set up on my own as a visiting hairdresser, going my rounds on a push bike, but this took time and I hoped for a motor-bicycle, to which my father strongly objected. So Bob Crampton found a second-hand Austin 7 for £25. I joined the A.T.S. in 1941. Indeed the previous day I crashed with the gas man, also driving an Austin 7, so I had to borrow a car in order to say Good-bye to my friends and clients and to give them a final 'hair-do' – these included the late Dr. and Mrs. Gordon-Jones and the late Captain Austin Turner and his family at Potters Hill.

The Night of the Air Raid

In September, 1940, while a darts match was in progress at
"The Royal Oak", Wrotham Heath, and the Bar was full of
customers, a German raider loosed a stick of 16 high explosive
bombs, the first of which scored a direct hit on the Inn, penetrating
the kitchen roof, killing my step-grandmother and a kitchen maid
called Mary Breed. Blast and splinters devastated the Bars, killing
and wounding customers, amongst whom were J. Mansell, F.
Whiteman and Fred Heines. Mr. George Sears had the distressing
experience of helping to remove the dead. Other bombs damaged
Rootes garage and several dwellings on the Sevenoaks Road, setting
alight a gas pipe on the outer wall of the Cafe now called "The
White Rose Restaurant", at that time known as Mrs. Roberts' Tea

Rooms, where so great was the heat that sweets melted in their bottles. On the opposite side of the road, three bombs fell on Wrotham Heath House, causing casualties and injuries.

That night I was on duty at Borough Green Civil Defence Post (Caxton House) as a sitting-case driver, and received a telephone call from the H.Q. at West Malling, with the news of the air raid at Wrotham Heath, but the exact position of the bomb damage was not given. I was however instructed to go to Wrotham Cottage Hospital, in order to collect nursing staff and to proceed to Wrotham Heath House for orientation. Here I found Dr. Green, Mr. Brian Champion, Warden for Wrotham, and Captain Austin Turner, Warden for Wrotham Heath, in charge. The house had received a direct hit and was in complete darkness; we had to use torches to find the dead and injured. As I was leaving the premises in order to return to the Civil Defence Post where Mrs. Noel Thomas was in charge, I heard that "The Royal Oak" had been hit, and I immediately thought of my parents. Mr. Champion offered to get me across the main road which was blocked, I found my father quite alright, and though covered with plaster and dust from head to foot, had taken command of the situation, and had organised the clearing and cleaning up, helped by my brother who happened to be at home on leave.

In "The Kent Messenger" the following was published: "Mr. and Mrs. John Swift were both uninjured, although shaken, everyone was high in their praise of the calmness and pluck with which they faced the situation. 'They were wonderful' said one of the customers. 'Mr. Swift had the presence of mind to turn off the gas and electricity and do everything he could under the circumstances'".

Note by John Geddes: The Royal Oak at Wrotham Heath was bombed by a German raider on Tuesday, October 13th 1940 at 9.30p.m. – a dull dark evening. The time of the incident was recorded by the clock in the Bar which stopped at the above hour. It was left lying there for some while after the raid.

The Royal Oak, Wrotham Heath, 1925

WROTHAM HEATH

Doris Hayes

Wrotham Heath has always been my home, having spent my childhood in No.3 Windmill Hill, and since my marriage to the late Arthur Hayes I have lived in No.1 Fir Tree Cottages – once the home of the Coachman to the late Lady Lowther of Wrotham Heath House.

One of my earliest memories at the age of 7, is accompanying the late Mrs. Costen (who died last year aged 96) when she was needed at Warren Wood, now the home of David Hyder, and at Wrotham Heath House in Lady Lowther's day, in order to give extra help with dinner parties and other formal occasions. It was a dark and lonely walk up to Warren Wood, through the woods, along a path behind the "Royal Oak", a small inn at that time, and I must have held Mrs. Costen's hand very tightly as we walked along by the light of a lantern on winter nights. Like so many local children, there was the daily walk up to the dairy at Great Comp, across Maxwell's Park (now Windmill Park) to fetch the milk; on one

90

occasion, whilst climbing the big oak tree at the entrance to the Park, I remember falling into a pond below.

The Mission Room, situated at the bottom of the hill, just below the railway (later destroyed by fire and now the site of two houses) was started in 1900 by the Miss Mansells of Nepicar Lodge, and the wife of Dr. Charlewood Turner of Warren Wood, this was an important feature of life in Wrotham Heath. It was used for occasional Services and Sunday School, which took place in a small adjoining room containing an altar and cupboards for hymn books, all of which were put away and the door closed and locked by Mrs. Emily Bish, the caretaker. The main part of the building provided accommodation for the local Men's Club meetings, wedding receptions, whist-drives, concerts and theatricals and other village activities.

At the age of 14 I went to work for Mrs. Roberts at the Tea Rooms, once the Post Office and now "The White Rose Restaurant", at 5/- per week, and at 18 I went to help at Woodlands, Platt, at that time the home of Brigadier Keane's family. In 1940 I joined the "WAAF's", eventually becoming Lance Corporal in the RAF station at Turnhouse, where I was in charge of Corporal's Mess. Later in the war, I joined the Land Army until my marriage.

Mr. Albert Bowen has kindly supplied information about Wrotham Heath before my day, since he was born in one of the

Forge Cottages in 1897 (See "Platt Parish Pump" for August 1977). He remembers "Pretty Cap" Broad, who lit the only street lamp each night on the Deals, the open space at the junction of A20 and A25. He also recalls buildings and dwellings in this area; the forge (now Bay Cottage) and Mr. Luxford (Senior) the blacksmith, his son and two daughters who subsequently kept a general store, where one could buy amongst many other things, the best selections of haberdashery it is possible to imagine, – Harmers, who started a bicycle shop and Banfield's small garage which moved to bigger

The Royal Oak and Post Office, Wrotham Heath. 1907, at junction of London and Sevenoaks roads, now A20 and A25

premises, later to become Rootes Garage – the village policeman, who lived in No.2 Marion Cottages, and Carlow's Bakers, (later

Thomsett's) at the corner of the main road and Windmill Hill. Nearby lived Hazeldene, (gardener to Lady Lowther) and his two daughters Ethel and Beryl, the latter still works at the "Royal Oak". Mr. Bowen recalls playing cricket on the main London to Maidstone road, using a large stone on the triangle of land known as "The Deals" as a wicket – later the site was occupied by an AA box.

CIVILIAN AND ARMY LIFE
Leonard Harmsworth

During the First World War we moved from Offham village to Offham level railway crossing, living in a house (recently demolished) where my father had charge of the gates and the goods yard, which was very well used, especially by local farmers, who sent their produce and hop-pockets by rail. About two weeks before hop-picking started, there would be hundreds of horse-drawn gypsey caravans using the crossing on their way to and from the hop-fields, all gaily painted, with gleaming brasswork.

We left the house after 5 or 6 years, owing to the disturbance caused by traffic at night. My father would be called out of bed perhaps a dozen times in one night to open the gates and let the traffic through, so we moved to Trottiscliffe. I remember my two brothers and I aged 6, 8 and 9 walking to Offham School. Our playmates there would give us metal objects, nails, keys, staples etc., which we placed on the railway line where the train would flatten them to the thickness of paper – our father was unaware of this. Sometimes when the goods train stopped to shunt the trucks out of the goods yard to leave empty ones, the train driver and his fireman would lift us up onto the engine, and we would travel to and fro during the shunting.

One incident I recall, my father had closed the crossing gates to let the train through, but as it was not in sight he allowed a woman and a small boy to cross the line by the wicket gate, a normal practice. Where the rails passed through the roadway there was a protecting rail to prevent stones piling up against the running-rail leaving a 1½ inch gap. The boy poked the toe of his shoe into this gap and became wedged; my father unable to free him, rushed back to the signal box and put the signal at red, my mother ran up the line with the red flag, the train tried to stop and was crossing the bridge over Seven Mile Lane, when my father managed to free the boy; the train could not have stopped in that short distance.

We would spend a week's holiday with relatives living on the Hadlow–Tonbridge Road, my brothers and I being sent ahead an hour or so before my parents who also walked carrying the luggage. In later years we had the use of a horse and trap from Jack Swift of the Royal Oak driven by a Mr. Underdown; it was quite safe then for small children to be sent unaccompanied on long journeys on foot. During the school holidays we went hop or fruit picking at 1/- a day. The nearest houses to the crossing at that time were the Tollgate opposite Rootes Garage, The Royal Oak, Warren Wood, Highlands Farm and the Golf Club House - during the First War there were two searchlights and a naval gun in a turret behind the

Club House. In the opposite direction were May Hill and the lodge gates to Addington Place, owned by Mr. Whitburne, whose horses were shod at Wrotham Heath Forge by Mr. Luxford and his son – see "Reminiscences by Albert Bowen" August 1977 Parish Pump. East of Askew Bridge on the Sevenoaks Road a narrow path leads to a rise known as Holly Mount, on which stood a farm house, the remains were still to be seen in 1950. This overlooked a cricket pitch which was partly shaded by chestnut trees, felled a few years ago to widen the road, the land is now a chicken farm.

In 1930 at the age of 17 I joined the Seaforth Highlanders, and after 6 months at Fort George near Inverness I was posted to Dover Castle where I spent a year before posting to Palestine, being stationed alternately at Haifa and Jerusalem with detachment duties in practically every town of any size in the country. We went by coach down to the Dead Sea for bathing; owing to the mineral salts in the water it was impossible to sink, and at a depth of 12ft. we could only submerge to chest level. We could roam around the hills and countryside as we wished. During the latter part of our stay there was much civil unrest, and road traffic had to move in convoy. I spent several weeks travelling between Haifa and Jerusalem as escort.

We then moved to Egypt to the Citadel in Cairo for two years, during which time we visited all the antiquities and pyramids, and trained out in the desert for weeks on end. We provided a guard for the Residency, the grounds of which ran down to the Nile. My favourite post was by the river, watching the boats sailing by; Cairo always had a peculiar smell of burnt cork. At Port Said we embarked for Hong Kong, passing through the Canal and going ashore at Columbo and Singapore. I was stationed at the Peak of Hong Kong for a year. In 1937 we experienced a severe typhoon and finally started the 5 weeks voyage home by troopship. Back home I was discharged, but soon recalled for 2 months' training and mobilised at the outbreak of World War II, going to France with the 51st Highland Division during the "Phoney War" the Winter of 1940.

In the Spring of 1940 two divisions at a time were sent to gain experience in the Outworks of the Maginot Line, and when the Germans attacked we became cut off from the BEF, and formed part of a French Army. I was taken prisoner near St. Valery after the French and German Armistice. We marched into Holland, and then were taken by barge down the Rhine to Dortmund, and thence by cattle truck to Thorn, in Poland, where I spent 5 years, working in a sugarbeet factory, and building prison camps for Russian prisoners who poured in during 1941. I ended up working on a farm until Christmas 1944, when we heard the rumble of the Eastern Front moving towards us. We were marched into a nearby town where 250 of us were assembled and with 40 guards to march North Westward. Scores of German troops attached themselves to our column, trying to return to their homes in Germany. We came to a road block where we waited until their Military Police sorted out which were guards and which were not. The first few weeks proved gruelling owing to thick snow and some 50 degrees of frost and lack of food and shelter. We left several men along the way in villages and local hospitals suffering from severe frostbite and other ailments. By the middle of April, we arrived in West Germany after many detours having marched nearly a thousand miles. We then started going back because of the approaching American Front, but a friend and I broke free and made our way towards the West, living off the land for 5 days, the countryside being hilly and wooded until we fell in with some German soldiers hiding in woods, who told us that the Americans had taken the nearby towns. So we made our way down the hill and contacted a group of tanks and were then sent to the British Zone, which flew us home, where after a few months I was discharged after 15 years of army life.

WALNUT TREE COTTAGE & ENVIRONS

Leonard Harmsworth

In 1947 I married Daisy Stratton of Walnut Tree Cottage, Wrotham Heath, where she had lived since a child and whose forbears had occupied this property for three generations. The cottage was at one time thatched – the chimney being reduced in height by two feet when the roof was slated. The walnut tree itself which over-shadowed the house was said to be the largest in Kent, probably 300 years old, since these trees were introduced during the 17th century. However, it had to be felled in 1955, the trunk measured 5ft across, and was bought by a timber merchant for £150, but as it proved to be hollow it was left there and we eventually sawed it up for firewood. I visited the Archives at County Hall, and thereby traced the history of our cottage and its former occupants, members of the Leney family, brewers who also owned the Brewery at Nepicar, a house still standing opposite the Moat Hotel, called "Old Brewery".

The land surrounding Walnut Tree Cottage was Common Land before the Enclosure Act, and was at one time owned by a Mr. Collins, who employed the squatters already living there in thatched bothies, whose livelihood was the cutting of brushwood from local woods; the land then passed to the Lambards and subsequently to the Nevill family. On the hill above our house is The Retreat, once a bothy, home of the Fitness family who have lived there for generations; I am told that one of their ancestors returned there from fighting at the Battle of Waterloo. Gallows or Galley Hill behind us, was the site of a Windmill, built about 1800 on an acre of land leased to William Luck from Richard James, Lord of the Manor of Wrotham. According to a Document, an Abstract of the title of the land – i.e. "A piece of land lying near Galley Hill, on which was erected a messuage and buildings and a windmill, formerly the Estate of John Saxby", since this land was subsequently held by Captain Randolph, whose name occurs on the Tithe map of 1840, the former may have been the Miller before that date, though no date can be given to one Parris in connection with the windmill. By 1880 it was out of use as such, and served as a store, and was finally burnt down early this century. Parris or one of his family operated Ford Mill, situated on the outskirts of the parish, and this water mill was most certainly on the site of the one first mentioned in the Addington Parish Records in 1472. The late Jack Hayes of Wrotham Heath told me of a photograph showing an arch over the road-way between the Mill and Ford Place, which would have been a viaduct carrying a supply of water to Ford Place, and returning to the stream lower down.

The main road from London to Hythe was previously via Farningham, Kingsdown, Stansted, Trottiscliffe, Addington, Larkfield, Aylesford and Penenden Heath. A loop went to Wrotham, Wrotham Heath, Offham and Maidstone, rejoining it at Penenden Heath. The earliest hop-pickers from London went through Stansted and Trottiscliffe stopping at The George Inn and then on to Addington, some taking the track leading into Valley Woods (now approached by the pathway under the railway bridge between the Royal Oak and the Rose Restaurant) along a track or old coach road leading to Mereworth. In Valley Woods apart from trenches dug by troops practising in the 1914 war, are traces of an ancient roadway, some of which have disappeared under the extension to the Golf Course. The thickness of top-soil deposited in its more shallow parts, determines its age, when it takes 100 years to form one inch of top-soil in a wood.

Provision was made in 1752 for the making up of the road from Wrotham to Wrotham Heath, presumably the first time it was fully metalled. In the course of a dispute over Rights of Way at Wrotham Heath in 1965, records showed that the track under the above-mentioned railway bridge was indeed part of an old coach road.

PLATT WOMEN'S INSTITUTE

J.V.C.Turner

It was In 1919, shortly after the first World War that Mrs.
Carine Cadby of Ruffway, who had organised a Red Cross working
group held in her house composed of local ladies, and who, when
these sewing parties ended, suggested that some form of social club
should take its place. Miss Olive Gilbert and Mrs. Belle Evans
remember a meeting at the Old School to which Mrs.
Heron-Maxwell (a pioneer of Women's Institutes in this country)
came and proposed that they should join the National Federation of
Women's Institutes.

Thus Platt W.I. came into being with Mrs. Cadby as its first
President, followed by Miss Somerville of Gt. Comp Oast, an
experienced producer of drama, later by Miss Bright, Headmistress
of Platt School, then Mrs. Todman of Oak Beams, succeeded in turn
by Mrs. Gerald McDermott of Brackenhill, Mrs. Fox of Huntsman's
Lodge, and Mrs. Peak of The Old Brewery, Nepicar. Miss Elsie
Pascall was elected secretary, and served in this capacity to three
Presidents. Happily, some of the Founder Members are still with us,

and from their excellent memories and photographs, much can be recorded, supplemented by minutes from 1924, kindly edited by Mrs. Langford, until recently President.

Various activities and classes are mentioned by Miss Gilbert: how to dry and cure rabbit skins with which to make gloves and moccasins, upholstery, cookery, basket and rug making and leather work classes. A produce stall in 1930 at Wrotham gave Platt first place with seven red stars. Occasional lantern slides were shown, and Mrs. Pyke and Miss Brooker would always oblige by singing comic songs. Mrs. Percy Minter of Staddleswood, the Choir Mistress, started a Singing Circle in her house, members of which sang part songs at W.I. meetings. Lessons in Country Dancing by Miss Carey, for which the women wore home-made ankle-length white dresses trimmed with yellow and green, the Institute colours, while those who took men's parts wore smocks, a craft learnt at meetings. A picked team of eight Country Dancers, including Miss Gilbert, competed in London, winning 3rd prize, which was presented by Princess Marie-Louise. A display also took place during the Church Fair, at that time held in Anchor Fields, now St. Mary's Close, as well as taking part in a big rally at Leeds Castle amongst other places.

Mrs. Belle Evans recalls successful productions of Shakespeare under the direction of Miss Somerville, "Mid-Summer Night's Dream" in the grounds of Stone Ridge, at that time the home of General Sir Arthur and Lady Linden-Bell. The trial scene from

"Henry VIII" in the communicating gardens of Staddleswood and Woodlands, two performances followed by a dance on the lawn. An Olde Time Fair took place in Wrotham Square under the direction of Miss Lally when Platt W.I. formed a company of strolling players, acting an old Cornish morality play, "Noah and his Ark", for which Miss Harrie Turner designed and made the animal heads; there is an excellent photograph of this showing many well-known faces of that time. Mrs. Evans also recalls a memorable occasion when the late Mr. Nettlefold of Wrotham Park, asked if Platt W.I. would entertain some of his theatrical friends, which included Dame Sybil Thorndyke and Dame Ellen Terry. He sent a large horse-drawn wagon to fetch the cast, and a scene from "Twelfth Night" was performed, for which they received high praise, and after a sumptuous tea were presented with a cheque for £5 by their host.

Miss Elsie Pascall also took part in many activities and classes, and remembers a special Christmas treat when entertainment was provided by some well-known people including Mable Constanduros and Helen Mellais. Subscriptions in the early days was 2/- per annum, and several members came from Borough Green until their own W.I. was formed. Outings to the seaside are recorded, garden meetings with stalls and entertainments, proceeds being given to Charity. There was a Folk Dancing Festival and demonstration of sword dancing, a produce and needlework stall operated at each meeting and in 1926 a cello was sold for 45/-. In that year the Post Office was successfully approached by the Institute with regard to the installation of a public telephone box near the Memorial Hall. In 1931 the cost of a visit to Lullingstone Castle for a coach holding 31 members was £2 1s 4d!

Miss Mary Somerville of Comp Oast

Early in 1940 the Merchant Service asked the Institute for knitted garments for their crews and 191 were made within 6 months. A Red Cross and Prisoner of War stall was successful in raising money for this purpose, as were Whist Drives. Rationing resulted in talks by Miss Petty, the 'Pudding Lady' who demonstrated different ways of preparing any food available, including 'Carrot Charlotte'.

During the war years, attendance was so low that there was a risk of closing down for the duration; however, after much heart searching and the result of a questionnaire, it was decided to keep going, and to have classes of 'Make Do and Mend', Needlework, Knitting and debates. Mrs. Langford, lately President, tells us that the format of the W.I. remains much the same as it was originally, though meetings are now held in the evenings since so many members have part-time jobs during the day.

Platt W.I. celebrated its Diamond Jubilee in 1979. In 1931 the motto: 'A merry heart goes all the way' was chosen – presumably this still holds good.

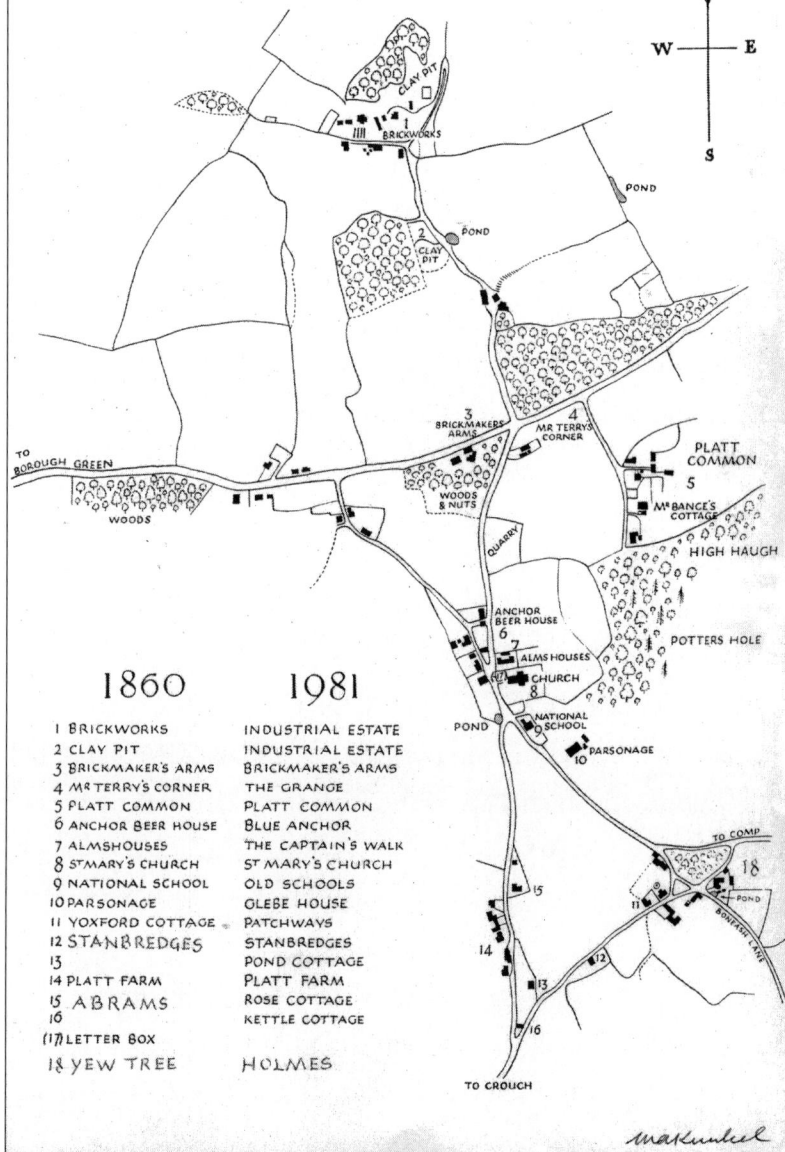

PLATT 1860

W   E

S

CLAY PIT

BRICKWORKS

POND

2
CLAY PIT

POND

3
BRICKMAKERS
ARMS

4
MR TERRY'S
CORNER

PLATT
COMMON

5

MR BANCE'S
COTTAGE

WOODS
& NUTS

TO
BOROUGH GREEN

WOODS

QUARRY

HIGH HAUGH

ANCHOR
BEER HOUSE

6

7

ALMS HOUSES

CHURCH

8

POTTERS HOLE

9
NATIONAL
SCHOOL

POND

PARSONAGE

10

TO COMP

18

POND

11

15

BONFFEAST LANE

14

12

13

16

TO CROUCH

1860	1981
1 BRICKWORKS	INDUSTRIAL ESTATE
2 CLAY PIT	INDUSTRIAL ESTATE
3 BRICKMAKER'S ARMS	BRICKMAKER'S ARMS
4 MR TERRY'S CORNER	THE GRANGE
5 PLATT COMMON	PLATT COMMON
6 ANCHOR BEER HOUSE	BLUE ANCHOR
7 ALMSHOUSES	THE CAPTAIN'S WALK
8 ST MARY'S CHURCH	ST MARY'S CHURCH
9 NATIONAL SCHOOL	OLD SCHOOLS
10 PARSONAGE	GLEBE HOUSE
11 YOXFORD COTTAGE	PATCHWAYS
12 STANBREDGES	STANBREDGES
13	POND COTTAGE
14 PLATT FARM	PLATT FARM
15 ABRAMS	ROSE COTTAGE
16	KETTLE COTTAGE
(17) LETTER BOX	
18 YEW TREE	HOLMES

THE WOODS

Leonard Harmsworth

Platt and Wrotham Heath have more woodland than most local villages. Valley Woods to the East and Platt Woods to the West, the latter with a path leading from Windmill Lane to the Church and another to Platt Common. At one time these woods would have joined with Hurst Woods, part of Wealden Forest. Some parts of the Valley Woods have been planted with chestnut which is felled every ten years for fencing, and some areas opened for farming such as the late Tom Ward's leading to the Golf Course.

Platt Woods have a varied mixture of trees, including the Wellingtonias, originally called the Giant Redwood, discovered in U.S.A., saplings of which were sent to Europe, each country giving their own particular name; in England they were called after the first Duke of Wellington.

These woods were landscaped in the mid-nineteenth century for Lady Caroline Nevill, who proposed to have a house built, in preparation for which the rhododendrons were planted and some of the conifers. However, this plan was abandoned when it transpired that the woods would be closed to the public, with the exception of the path leading to the Church on Sundays, but firmly shut after Evensong by the keeper. Within living memory this function was taken over by a formidable man called Crouch. Betty Gibson says that one only had to pick a leaf for Crouch to appear, let alone rhododendron flowers, which are an incredible sight, especially in Potters Hole. There is no record how this became so called; if it was an excavation, it must be centuries ago, since there are no abrupt sharp edges. The name is shown on maps of 1568, 1860 and on the Apportionment Roll of 1840. I recall in 1920 when with my mother and brothers we were picnicking in the woods, and were confronted by Crouch who told us that the only place where we could sit was on the foot-path which led from the Common to Windmill Lane.

On the Ordnance map of 1820 this lane, which now starts below the railway bridge at Wrotham Heath, was only a narrow one, as far as the windmill marked 'Comp Corn Mill' on the right, and serving on the left the cottages, one group of which housed the groom and some of the staff from Addington Place, and another for the navvies about to excavate for the railway, with a detached house, probably a farm dated 1785. Up beyond the Mill was undivided woodland (see map of Wrotham Heath 1820, page vi). There are two bridle paths running through the Valley Woods from Wrotham Heath, as well as traces of older roads; we find evidence of these ancient ways mainly in woodland, because in open country they were quickly obliterated by farming and enclosure. In a dispute over

Rights of Way some 20 years ago, a map from the British Museum showed a road going under the railway bridge at Wrotham Heath, across the Golf Links and joining the Offham-Teston road and thence on to Mereworth.

A house in the Woods by S Vinson

In the Valley Woods near the path from Windmill Lane to the Links, there are remains of about 100 yards of old track way, we know it is old because of the tree stumps in the bottom and the absence of excavated soil. There was another stretch of trackway recently obliterated by extending the Golf Course, both these could have been the same track which joined the one coming from the bottom of Windmill Hill.

During the First World War, troops practised trench digging, easily recognised, and wood cutting was done by the army in Platt Woods during that period (see page 3, K. Rogers).

In the past, woods were made more use of than now, since in the days when every dwelling had a brick-built copper and the washing was done on a Monday, there would be a succession of local inhabitants going to and fro, collecting bundles of firewood from the woods to boil the coppers. I myself, when small, helped my aunt in Offham woods, half the village seemed to be there!

PLATT WOODS' CONTRIBUTION TO THE 1914-18 WAR

Kenneth Rogers

Wars help to form a major part of the history of most countries, England being no exception. The 1914-18 war is part of that history and also the history of Platt.

There were shortages of many things, timber being one of them. The owners of Platt Woods called for tenders for buying up some of the trees and Mr. L. Curtis of Curtis & Caine (now known as F. P. Caine Ltd.) met their agent and went through the wood marking trees which should not be felled. Mr. Curtis then took me up to the site and instructed me to measure up the fir trees to be cut down. I had to measure the height and girth of each tree, under supervision on the first day, marking each tree with a specially made cutting knife. Finally, at the office I had to work out the total cubic feet of useful timber in the whole of the wood. The firm then sent in their tender price which was accepted.

Then came, to me, the exciting part. The firm purchased the necessary machinery to do the work, a very large steam engine which was sited at Potters Hole, saw benches, moving roller racks, large and small circular saws etc., including felling axes and two-handed saws for felling the trees. A large open sided shed was then built over the engine and benches, a mess hut for the men and an office hut. The trees were felled the branches cut off and the main trunks pulled to

Platt Woods by William Cadby

the mill at Potters Hole by an enormous stallion. Mr. Ladhams was in charge of the horse which was stabled in a building at the Brick Yards. After a short while Mr. Ladhams gave up the horse, as he was rather a small man he found the animal too much for him and Mr. Gasson took over the job and became very attached to him.

Mr. Sam Hankinson, the firm's foreman painter, became foreman of the mill. A Mr. Cox, an elderly man from Sevenoaks, was in charge of the engine, he having been a ship's engineer.

Many men and women of Platt worked on this enterprise. There was a donkey called 'Beauty' lent by Mr. A. E. Collings, that pulled the twigs to a clearing under the care of one of the women and then the twigs etc. were burnt, the remaining ashes being used by the farmers as potash. The branches were sawn up and made into pitprops of various sizes and sold either to the army for use in the trenches, or to the coal mines. The main trunks were sawn into planks, 2" x 3" and 2" x 4" etc. sizes and sent in trucks by rail to London timber merchants and were eventually used for repairs to bomb damaged dwellings or for use generally in the building works. Huge piles of sawdust were collected by army wagons for use in bedding for their horses. The bark was sawn off about 1" thick in slabs and used by the army for making huts for the men. Jack Reville was one of several men working on cutting the pitprops.

It was arranged that when the armistice came a blast was sounded on the whistle of the Mills engine and everyone had the rest of the day off. The work continued for some while after the end of the war.

SOME THOUGHTS ABOUT PLATT WOODS

Mary Anne Kunkel
(formerly Charlewood Turner)

It is quite astonishing how one can know a place well and yet find, familiar though it is, that one hasn't really seen it properly, – until suddenly, a chance remark will make one sit up and take notice of things which had somehow been overlooked before. After fifty years Platt Woods revealed themselves to me in such a way; I was indeed very much astonished.

As children, adolescents and grown-ups we have run about, and then more sedately walked or wandered through the Woods, and so by now we really should know every inch of them, and of course all about the plants and animals too. However, when I tried to write a description of Platt Woods I found that I didn't in fact know much about them at all; except that there are lots of Rhododendrons, and a good many Scots Firs; that there are places where Sweet Chestnuts grow, and also that Silver Birches and the good old Oaks are quite common. Then there are those marvellous Beech trees at the top of the path up from the Church, and the pair of even bigger ones on the slopes above Roughacres where usually there is a swing-rope hanging down from a great high branch which always made me wonder how it got up there. All in all not much to base some writing on. It was time to go for a walk up in the woods and to have a good look around.

We say "up" because The Woods are on a little hill of their own and part, so I understand, of the long ridge of upper-green-sand which runs parallel to the chalk of the North Downs. This soil is sandy as we all know, and quite different from the soil down in Platt where suddenly the Rhododendrons cease to grow so happily. I am sure that whoever planted the "rhodadendrums" in the first place could have had no idea how much they would spread; allowed to grow unchecked they would eventually take total possession, and lovely as they are when in flower a whole forest of them would be too much of a good thing. So the difficult work of clearing and cutting back is essential to preserve Platt Woods as a mixed woodland. In this way many new paths have been made recently, and each time I go up into the Woods I seem to discover a new one. It is nice to follow these different paths into bits of the Woods which before had been all blocked up by impenetrable thickets; and at one time even the two main tracks were in danger of being overgrown.

As kids we considered paths to be rather unnecessary and found it much more fun to flounder, crawl or wriggle through the darkly mysterious entanglements of the Rhododendrons, returning home to Potters Hill extremely black and grubby from these satisfactory explorations, especially after looking for badgers at the old sets in Potters Hole. I haven't been down there for a long time; I wonder if the holes still exist?

Nearby (in Potters Hole) grow two Wellingtonia trees, rising straight and tall above the surrounding woodland. One wonders how they came to be planted just there, and why, and by whom? It is said that the Nevills planned to build a house somewhere in the area; it is intriguing to imagine how these woods would have looked at that time. Evidently the Nevills thought that the place needed some improvement... hence the planting of trees other than native kinds: the Wellingtonias, the cypress, thuyas and of course the rhododendrons.

Perhaps Potters Hole was "landscaped" into a garden of beautiful different coloured rhododendrons, the Wellingtonias and who can tell what else besides, but now long since overgrown. The site of the proposed house might have been on the other side of the wood where the groups of cypress, thuyas and two more Wellingtonias are to be found. Were the larches along the top path planted too? – and what about the Scots firs? Once one begins to ask such questions more and more come following on...

What did the original woodland look like? Today we have growing there wild native species like oak and birch and beech. And the holly, is this "native" too? The rowan ash, elder and whitebeam grow there now, did they always do so? Hazel and hawthorn are to be found round edges of the wood and are no doubt "run-wild" hedgerow species and as such do not belong in the woods. The sweet chestnuts would have been planted for coppicing presumably at the same time as the Valley Woods and Hurst Woods were planted up. When exactly this was I can only hazard a guess that it might have been during the first world war (see page 3, K. Rogers) when a lot of the Scots fir would have been felled for pit-props and the like. Firs grow slowly so the fast growing chestnut would have been the obvious alternative. Eighty or so years ago there might have been many more fir trees than there are today, but no chestnuts.

What is really needed is the gift of travel backwards in Time! For example, I'd like to see it all as it was before the Romans came...

Rhododendrons & Beech

a primaeval forest of oak with wolves, bears and wild boar? Because of the lighter soil there would perhaps have been a less dense forest than down in the valleys and therefore more accessible for humans. But no streams of water flow through or anywhere particularly nearby, so probably no-one went to live there until piped water was laid on in the 20th century!!! Down in Platt and round about all you had to do was to dig a well, and that is where until surprisingly little time ago everyone's water came from. But up on that green-sand the water all drains away and so there being neither ponds or streams on record, no larger animals would have actually lived there, they would just have been passing through, hunting or being hunted, depending on who they were. But perhaps there were more streams and ponds in those days. There certainly are several permanently "soggy" spots.

But now, and rather luckily for us, the wild life of Platt Woods appears to consist of nothing more alarming than some cheeky grey squirrels, some wood-pigeons and an unimpressive number of smaller birds, and perhaps a passing fox or two; has anyone seen a badger up there lately? In all, few animals, or maybe having more of an eye for plants I have not noticed the creatures. It is said that in the days when the Nevills owned the place, they had a game keeper to look after things, and that one reason for planting the rhododendrons was as cover for the pheasants. Today the most likely "creature" to meet is another inhabitant of Platt with dog or two, also going for a walk. There can't be much to interest a dog... no rabbits, foxes or badgers to hunt after; and for people no fear of adders or other creepy-crawlies as there are in the Hurst Woods where grass snakes and adders are not uncommon.

Each season has its delights...for example a wet autumn following a hot summer usually produces a fascinating variety of fungi of different kinds, and some mushrooms are edible; so persons who know about such subjects may find the autumn the best time for the woods with its special smells of leaf mould, stink-horns or dog stink-horns – 'mutinus caninus' – and the ripening of chestnuts, beech mast and acorns.

Winter is muddy, as I seem to remember...quagmires of a kind of porridge of mushed up old black leaf-mould, and the leaves of the rhododendrons always seem wet and shower one with water even if it is not actually raining. All is grey then, grey misty-foggy air, grey tree trunks, the bracken turned grey-brown on a grey day, but is bright and golden on a sunny day; the woods become semi-transparent, one can see the network patterns of branches and twigs. It can be utterly quiet on those early darkening days. Or wild and exciting on a stormy day when the wind rushes through the tree tops, hissing and roaring, so one might imagine oneself at sea, eyes shut listening only... but don't get blown over!

Spring is lovely, the fiddle-heads of bracken uncurl from the deep layers of last year's leaves, and the trees put on a filmy dress of the most delicate colours, no more to begin with than a mere see-through garment of opening buds. Then comes June, and that is the special time for these woods to show off... when the rhododendrons are in full flower, nearly all mauve-pink now, but here and there a different kind of pink or a nearly red one, and the occasional white with dark spotted centre.

High summer can be anything from soggily-wet-heavy-green to toasted dry. In a drought the rhododendrons droop their foliage and the woods hum with summer insects, the fir-cones go "click", and the air is fragrant with the smell of resin and sun-heated bracken fern; there is the danger of fire, one cigarette can set the place alight. The coolest places are in and amongst the rhododendrons or under the spreading shade of a big beech tree.

These woods are so much part of my childhood, youth, and, well... really of my life, past, present and future all rolled into one that it is difficult to describe the place objectively. And missing here are lists of plants, animals and insects. However, the accompanying drawings of the leaves of the main trees which grow there now may be useful and serve as a guide not only to the present Platt Woods but also to their past and future too. I have found this subject more and more interesting, and there is more and more to wonder about. Everything has a history of some sort; there is always a world concealed, the thing is, to go and have a look, unearth it as it were.

PLATT WOODS

Freda Cross

Many of the present-day residents of Platt might be surprised to learn that Platt Woods of which they are so justly proud, did not belong to them at all before 1959. They were in fact owned by a "faceless" gentleman called Mr. Bradley, who suddenly decided to try and make some money out of them, and build a housing estate. Yet this is in fact was the case.

Three local men, Derek Benbow, representing Platt on the Rural District Council, Peter Doran, a County Councillor, and Brian Cross, Chairman of Platt Parish Council, supported by our Parish Council, got together to arouse public opinion. Mr. Bradley's application was not granted and his plan was foiled, but he still wanted a sum of £1500, far less of course than he would have got from his previous plan.

Once more, our three friends got busy and a meeting was held in Platt Memorial Hall on 30th March 1960, to which pretty well the whole village came, and half the sum, £750, was collected, even sixpences and pennies, from rich and poor. Malling R.D.C. agreed

to pay the other half, if Platt Parish Council would be responsible
for the maintenance. And so the Freehold was acquired, and Platt
Woods were safe, thanks to the tireless efforts of these three men, all
of whom have since died.

The Parish Council presented two seats as a memorial to
them, and a token of gratitude. One of the seats is in the
Churchyard on the left-hand side of the West door of Platt Church,
the other is at the top of the bank where the footpath through the
Churchyard enters Platt Woods, together with the steps and the
handrail.

THE HIGHWAYMAN

Diana Barton

One late afternoon in February, I was on my grey horse, going home through Hurst Woods, after a long ride across country. It was beginning to get dark, and a damp evening with melting snow lying at the edges of the path, so as we cantered slowly down the ride my horse's hooves were making a heavy splashing sound.

Just before we turned a corner leading into the old road to Tonbridge, my horse pricked up his ears and whinnied, so I was not surprised to see another rider ahead of us. It was a man on another grey horse followed by a whippet and he cantered before us in the dusk. I noticed immediately that he was wearing a long black coat which divided and blew behind him as he rose, and that his hat was on an odd old-fashioned shape. I then realised that I could hear no sound of the horse's hooves as he moved ahead. I pulled my horse up and looked down, and there were no hoof marks on the wet and snowy ground. The man had cantered on and disappeared into the gloom.

Sometime later, I read a local history and found that there had been a man who lived with his brother at Royden Hall, and had been convicted as a Highwayman. After dining at home, he used to change his clothes and hold up and rob the guests who had been to dinner. One of the clues that helped to convict him was the fact that he was always accompanied by his whippet dog. He was executed, and is reputed to be buried outside the wall of Royden Churchyard at East Peckham.

Several other riders have seen this apparition. I saw him once again myself; I was riding down a hill in the far side of Hurst Woods, and he galloped by very fast, on the track at the foot of the hill.

"REMINISCENCES OF AN OLD FREE TRADER"

by the late John Terry F.R.G.S.
(pub. 1888)

Free Traders or Smugglers of the eighteenth and early nineteenth century were not persons to be despised by their neighbours. and are referred to here as those gentlemen who avoided the Duty imposed by the Law. There is a clear connection between the 'Free Traders' of Wrotham and what was known to them as the Wood Street business in the City of London. Wrotham was the home of some of these men who made this village their head centre, for it was the last halt on the road from Deal, Romsey and Sandwich, en route for London.

Immediately above Wrotham village on the Downs is 'Old Terry's Lodge', formerly a mansion and estate, now a hamlet of a few cottages known as "Old Terry's". Close by was the site of the chief Beacons where the old Traders (or smugglers) had their telegraph station, a large scaffoldlike erection of timber with great plank arms, nearly as large as the arms of a windmill; these were pulled up or down, to the right or left, 2 or 3 at a time in various positions, similar to the semaphore signals on railways nowadays.

This telegraph station was in the line of vision of another at Shooter's Hill and at Boxley Hill. Those Free Traders in Wood St., London, receivers of tobacco, laces and spirits (known as 'Old Weeds', 'Old Rope Yarn' and 'Old Dusty') were fairly safe but had to pay smartly at times when things were traced to them. News of the presence of Excise or Preventive men was 'telegraphed' to the men on the Downs by different formations of cattle; for "caution, don't be seen", three cows or horses would be tethered together in various ways (see J. Terry page 23, Part 1). At night time the low house on the Downs showed a light at one end or both ends or in three places. Some fifty horses could be mustered with neighbours 'Old Gates', 'Old Catcher' and others at Ightham, Wrotham Heath and Crouch, sometimes 200 for a big run. The regular meeting-place was where Platt Grange now stands, at that time the land was common or waste land. The men involved were not wholly dependent on horses, since they also used dog-carts – a splendid pair of large, strong dogs which had made the journey many times and knew the way perfectly – one of the dogs whose home was at Wrotham Heath would run with one whose home was the Marsh, and visa versa, a method of travel so swift that not infrequently the old stage-coaches were overtaken by these 'canine carriers' and the quickest mode of despatching news to the 'front'.

Landing on the coast took place according to signs given on 'Flashers', a sort of pistol without a barrel, it has a flint lock and a pan to contain ¼ thimble-full of powder, a good stock of which was always carried in powder-horns, approximately 4 inches long, to fit into a waist-coat. On the return inland from the coast the gang broke up for their various 'hides' to dispose of their stuff, a suitable one was Wrotham Heath, a good position for watching the 'telegraph' system, with nothing to break the view to Hurst Woods, Crouch, along Ightham Common and Caesar's Camp (now Oldbury). In fact every smuggler seemed to have permission to hunt for rabbits anywhere, they deterred the poachers, and ladies of some houses encouraged their hidings so as to avail themselves of purchasing something without Duty, even the Squire was not too anxious to know how tobacco, silk handkerchiefs, etc. came into his possession.

The kitchen folk were all in favour to those men who brought tea, silk and others things in his pack, under his coat-tails or a petticoat with a large pocket or bladder containing the finest Brandy or Hollands. On one occasion some 20 horses with a swag consisting of kegs (holding 4 gallons each) and bales of silk weighing 50lbs each, were tracked down by the 'Preventive' men who traced the stuff to an old sand quarry at Platt stored in a shed known as a 'Thatched Down', a shed with thatched sides. Extra men, however, were needed from the Barracks in Maidstone, meanwhile the smugglers working at the back of the lodge made a hole large enough to pass small packages out, which were quickly carried up into Potter's Hole and there placed in another 'Hide'.

One driver 'Old Twiggs' drove a wagon to London with 'brooms', the reason for this kind of conveyance for illicit goods was the fear of being overhauled by the Preventive or Excise men, or by Highwaymen, who though shy of molesting a 'Trader', if this did happen, no mercy would be shown. The destination was Crosskeys Yard in Old Wood Street, London, a Brew House and Spirit Depot to which a great many loads of brooms used to go. The journey back with a large gang was simple, as the empties were slung under the wagon as though they were worthless, though containing London Porter for a neighbour who kept a coaching house at Wrotham Heath.

The shelter was the Great Hurst Wood, now the Valley Woods, adjoining Wrotham Heath, where their friends who lived in and around that area and who worked for them, professing to carry on the trade of Broom-dashers or Broom-makers of the Birch and Broom boughs for the London trade, since bass-brooms were unknown at that time. Large stacks of boughs lay scattered about in the woods, where a 'Hide' could be made for silks and such-like since the soil was sandy. These men were a strong and numerous lot, who had no employers, each one trading for himself in brooms for the 'FreeTrade', and could leave their broom-making at any moment to share in a run; they were however considered to be the rough or working element of the job, sometimes on the sea-shore, and liable to be victims of blood-shed and being 'pressed' by press-gangs and taken to sea.

N.B. After Waterloo a much stricter watch was kept by the Excise or Preventive men, round the coast, and punishment was much more severe. A "Smugglers Act" was passed in 1736, though its severity was mitigated in 1781 and 1784 which however increased the 'Free Trade' up to 1826 when all severities were re-imposed, and from that date Free-Trade or Smuggling was a failure.

(By courtesy of Mrs. Freda Cross)

FRANCES MARY HERON – MAXWELL

1864 - 1955

J.V.C. Turner

Frances Mary Cockburn was the 5th daughter of Admiral Cockburn of West Lothian, and on her marriage to Patrick Heron-Maxwell she lived at Dun Cree, Mount Stewart, a wedding present from her husband's parents, and their home until coming to Great Comp, which they bought from the Hon. Ralph Nevill in 1903.

Known to her friends as 'Max', Mrs. Heron-Maxwell was a formidable lady, somewhat masculine in appearance, with short cropped hair, dressed invariably in "useful" tweeds, a blouse and tie and an old Henry Heath 'Trilby' hat. This costume never varied whether she was chairing a committee meeting or on important occasions, not even the colour of the tweed, the exception being a black suit, white shirt and black tie for evening wear. Occasionally she was seen riding a bicycle wearing 'Bloomers' which shocked the locals. With the Heron-Maxwells from Scotland came their bailiff, James Geddes and his wife and family who settled in The Lodge (now called 'Old Comp') opposite the entrance to Great Comp; of their six children John Geddes the eldest son and his sister Elizabeth (now Mrs. Bird of Sevenoaks) are happily still with us, and a mine of valuable information and memories.

Mrs Heron-Maxwell of Great Comp

In those days The Park, or Maxwell's Park (now Windmill Park) was an open space vividly described by John Geddes on page 9. Part 1. Here local cricket matches were played, Girl Guides had their camps, and celebrations were held, such as that in honour of the Coronation of George V (see Stanley Box page 33).

On the estate at Great Comp worked three full-time gardeners Messrs. L. Eastwood of Comp Corner, Tom Stevenson succeeded by J. Fishenden of Bird's Field and Hayes of The Botha. There was a man in charge of the orchards by name of Reeves and an odd-job man from Offham, Mick Marchant. In the dairy where butter and cheese were made, Mr. and Mrs. Hayward were in charge, assisted by young Elizabeth Geddes, who later became part-time cook, when help was needed in the big house. Indoor staff consisted of the cook, Miss E. Bray, a kitchen maid, A. May, followed by Pet of Offham, a personal maid, E. Pullen and two other maids, Grace Digby and Hinton. Daily help came from Mrs. Alex Terry, who had been employed at Great Comp before Mr. and Mrs. Heron-Maxwell's time, and who continued to work there, a very well-liked resident of Platt Common.

Mrs. Heron-Maxwell was a strict mistress and told her staff that it was an honour to be a servant, to which one young maid replied: 'You give me your money and you can have my honour', a remark which resulted in her dismissal.

During the second war when labour was difficult to obtain, Mrs. Asdowne of Whatcote helped in various ways and was expected to arrive punctually at 7 a.m. in order to take early morning tea to the master and mistress. E. Vidler, wagoner and ploughman was in charge of the horses, and a large silver cup won by Mr. Heron-Maxwell in a steeplechase during his bachelor days was placed on the dining-room table on special occasions; in a corner of that room was a small staircase leading to the attics where the maids slept. It was up there that the trunks and travelling cases were kept. James Geddes, apart from his duties as Bailif was responsible for having these brought downstairs, polished and cleaned at least three weeks before the Heron-Maxwells left for a holiday. He also had charge of boot and shoe cleaning, sharpening and cleaning of knives, the weekly pay being [figure not given].

Mrs. Heron-Maxwell was an ardent Suffragette, and her activities and interests were many. When the West Kent Ladies' Hockey Association was formed in 1907 she became its Captain and subsequently President, finally in 1913 she was President of the All England Women's Hockey Association; she was also responsible for The Pilgrim's Club, playing in goal. Home matches took place on private grounds adjoining the house, cricket matches on a separate pitch which had been used for sheep during the winter, and when moved, their droppings provided valuable manure for tomatoes. In 1908 a cricket pavilion was given by Mr. Heron-Maxwell, this was used as a Department for packing the uniform of the Women's

Land Army during the second war, and is now a private dwelling.

Mrs. Heron-Maxwell's greatest achievement was surely the formation in 1918 of The West Kent Federation of Women's Institutes, and under her chairmanship various programmes were arranged, including the planning of Nursery Schools and village kitchens, and by 1920 fifty-eight Women's Institutes had been formed with 4,000 members, one of whom, Miss Mary Somervill, took an active part. She lived in Comp Oast (now Lambard's Oast) a born and gifted craftswoman, expert in spinning and weaving. and with Mrs. Heron-Maxwell produced plays and pageants acted by local inhabitants. She also learnt the craft of pottery from Henry Knipe. In 1919 Mrs. Heron-Maxwell proposed that Platt W.I. should join the National Federation of Women's Institutes, but being a very outspoken lady, did she perhaps have the habit of suggesting that she and only she was coping completely with the organisations she espoused? Differences of opinion and difficult situations occurred, and her forbidding appearance, unable to suffer fools gladly, hid acts of great kindness, an example of which is remembered by John Geddes when his father, the Bailiff died and her distress was so great that after a visit to his widow she was unable to attend the funeral.

With all her activities, surely Mrs. Heron-Maxwell's name will always be remembered in connection with the formation of the West Kent Federation of Women's Institutes, a great lady of "The Old Sort".

STROLLING PLAYERS OF 1927

Olive Gilbert

The photograph above shows the cast of a Cornish Morality play: "Noah and his Ark", which was performed by members of Platt Women's Institute, produced by Miss Somerville and Miss Lally as part of a medieval pageant by the combined Women's Institutes of Platt, Borough Green and Wrotham in 1927. This took place in Wrotham Square, since being a Chartered Town it was entitled to hold a Fair. Platt acted the parts of Strolling Players, who went from Fair to Fair; they entered the Square from the Maidstone Road, past the Bull Hotel, and placed their Ark on the base of the Church steps.

The cast consisted of:

Miss Harrie Turner	No. 9	The Voice of God
Miss Ann Brooker	No. 11	Doubting Thomas
Miss Olive Gilbert	No. 5	Noah
Mrs. Nora Collings	No. 3	Shem
Mrs Belle Evans	No. 10	Ham
Mrs Masters	No. 8	Japhet
Mrs Fletcher	No. 6	Wife of Shem
Mrs Box	No. 4	Wife of Ham
?		Wife of Japhet
Mrs Pyke	No. 7	Mrs. Noah
Miss Day	No. 2	?
Miss Amy Kidd	No. 1	?

Costumes and animal heads were made by Miss Somerville and Miss H. Turner, and the performance was judged by Dame Edith Craig (daughter of Dame Ellen Terry) who sat in a farm wagon placed across the road to Borough Green, from which traffic was halted.

HOLLEBON'S

Mary Gladdish

I was born at the home of my grandparents, 2 Wood Cottages, Platt, and I can well remember the little shop that was situated at the side of the cottage and some of the people who were customers. There was a Mr. Fado Laddams and a Mr. Ashdown both of Whatcote Cottages, and Mr. and Mrs. Bartholomew affectionately known as "Mr. and Mrs. Mom" to us small children; they lived just down the road at 6 Sabraon Villas, there were lots of others far too numerous to list. The hours of opening were somewhat flexible – from very early in the morning – to serve the men on their way to work, until quite late in the evening. Should the shop have been closed for any reason, a call of "shop" from the prospective customer was always answered cheerfully and they were served at no matter what time.

Local lads congregated in the shop during evenings and weekends to drink a variety of mineral waters. Hot drinks were sold during the winter – these were raspberry and black-currant cordials and a hot peppermint drink was made by my grandmother, Mrs. "Polly" Hollebon.

Mr. John Geddes who knew my grandparents well has helped by supplying the following information, and I quote: "Mr. Hollebon's shop was open every day and Mrs. Hollebon did her share of serving by leaving indoor work; both were always willing

Mrs 'Polly' Hollebon, formerly Mary Wolfe, grandmother of Mrs. Mary Gladdish.

to oblige and anything wanted would be ordered. Stock included soap, soda, vinegar (which was sold loose and kept in a barrel in an outhouse at the back of the cottage), condiments, Woodbine cigarettes 1d for 5, Will's Gold Flake and John Player's 3d for 10, pipe tobacco, shag and cigarette papers. Sweets included toffee 4ozs for 1d, bon-bons, aniseed roll and balls, Cupid's Whispers, Fry's chocolate cream bars 1d each and home-made ice-cream at 1d per cornet. Soft drinks included lemonade, ginger beer, "monster" bottles of mineral waters and in winter hot drinks of peppermint, black currant and raspberry juice. Customers, often those walking to work at Basted Mill, would call for oddments, shoe-laces, Batchelor's Buttons, hobnails and Blakeys for their own shoe repairs, and where "Harry" kept all his stock was a mystery and amazed everyone."

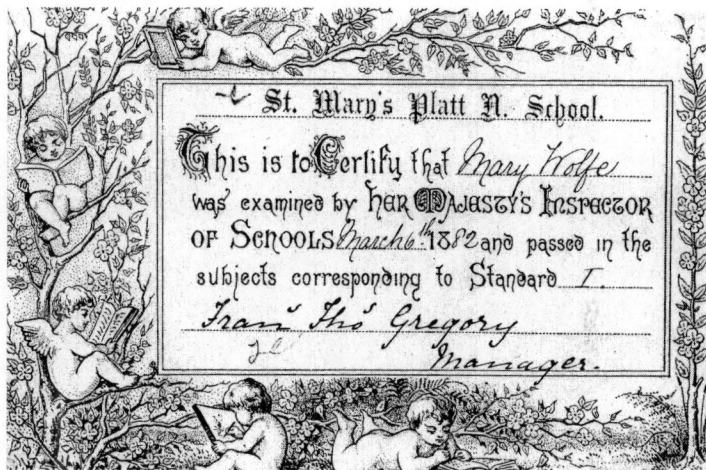

Mary Wolfe, grandmother of Mrs. Mary Gladdish.

Grandmother was a very jovial person with a great love for children and animals. I feel I should mention her dog "Jim", an old mongrel who scrounged goodies from the customers and was known to go to the cinema in Borough Green with the young people. On Sundays Jim used to go to Chapel in Borough Green with the late Mr. Charlie Evans and his sister Rosie and brother Albert who lived at "Dalesfield" – he was allowed to sit on the mat inside the door until the service was over and then return to Platt.

Hollebon's Shop

I would also like to include the story of Mrs. Blue Tits which was written by the late Miss Hewitt and printed in the Parish magazine; "Mrs. Hollebon, a lady who appeared vast, but I suspect most of her size was accounted for by her voluminous petticoats, with rosy cheeks and bright dark eyes and hair brushed straight back into a tight bun. She was pegging a child's shopping basket on to the clothes line, talking soothingly to an agitated parent blue-tit perched on the wash-house guttering. Then I saw that the basket was full of blue-tit babies, all very damp and noisy; they had been washed out of the Pump head by a heavy storm and Mrs. Hollebon was hanging them up to dry. The family, survived swinging happily on the clothes line when it was dry weather but pegged up in the wash-house when cold and wet."

Sadly due to the death of my grandfather, the outbreak of the second war and sweet rationing, it was necessary to close the little shop which was so much a part of Platt. I can't remember unfortunately and don't have any records of when the "shop" was first in existence, but do know it was there when my grandparents came to live here in 1903.

JIM PIKE

Harriette Niell

James Pike, a Hampshire man, went to Birling and became Head Gamekeeper to the Hon. Ralph Nevill of Birling Manor; when King George V was a guest for a shoot, Jim was his loader: "He was a nice gentleman, and a fine shot" was Jim's verdict.

Elizabeth Ann of Birling was the eldest of the 7 children of Tom Sharp, well-known as "The Kentish Thatcher"; she married Jim in 1905, but the lonely life of a game-keeper living in a cottage miles away from anywhere and anyone was not good for her, so Jim gave up his career and came to live here in Platt in No. 1 Church Cottages (now Hazel Cottage) – see picture overleaf. Of their four children, the only survivor is Mrs. Jenny Pott of The Lodge, Commenden Manor, Cranbrook, who has kindly contributed her memories of this remarkable man, who went to work on the local railway as linksman, a job he must have hated, though he was never heard to complain. They had a real country garden, there are very few such today, where he grew vegetables and flowers, kept chicken and bred canaries and was known as the local vet, his knowledge of herbs for curing complaints was remarkable. Mrs. Pike was a member of the 'Mother's Union' and is still remembered for her famous talk on how to trim a hat with cob-nuts, and her comic turns at meetings of Platt Women's Institute with Mrs. Kitney. She was an ingenious woman, who in order to attend a funeral service suitably clad, took an old black umbrella to pieces, with which she covered her hat and the collar and cuffs of her grey coat. She died on their Golden Wedding Day in 1955 aged 83. Jim lived for another ten years, and died in 1966 aged 92.

Mr & Mrs Jim Pike (outside 1 Church Cottages, now Hazel Cottage)

Those of us who had the pleasure of Jim Pike's friendship are the poorer by his death. Through his many troubles, he never complained; he had a zest for life and a capacity for happiness; his courage in adversity was unbounded. He had a very great knowledge of all wild things in this county and could tell stories of his game-keeping days with fascinating detail, and a gift of speech that brought the incident to life. He was a real country-man, an oaken heart

THE STEEPLE JACK

F. Bennett

Platt did at one time have a Steeple Jack, his name was Alec John Summers who was my grandfather. Alec came from the Mills in Lancashire where he learnt his trade and his parents owned a Mill.

Alec left Lancashire to build two steeples in Tovil for Mr. William Monckton, and came to Basted in 1875 with the Monckton family and built two steeples there and also all the new buildings on the Winfield side of the Mills: Calender House, Cutting Machines, Packing and Sorting Depots and Canteen.

Two of his sons he trained to be stonemasons, Alec and Tom. Grandfather was well-educated and was referred to by Mr. Monckton as 'Gentleman Jack' and Tom as 'Bossman' for Bosses man. He was a favourite of the Moncktons and did a lot of stone work at Ightham Warren for them. Every shaft or steeple Grandfather built he put initials A.J.S. on the bottom edge of some bricks to prove his work.

His sons also had and kept secret their own made formula for lagging and sealing the boilers. In 1923 August Bank Holiday week, the boilers had to be 'chipped' and the shafts cleaned out and inspected from the inside, a yearly event. It was a well known fact that when after the cleaning of the shaft was completed, the men celebrated with a drink and Grandfather did a 'Tap Dance' on the mortar board at the top of the shaft.

Platt Mill Employees – 1920

Top Row R.D. Sales, Snr. M. Gascoine, Snr. J. Evans G. Bennet (proprietor)
J. Huckstep Father Bartholomew Butcher, Snr. Bill Bartholomew G. Box, Snr.
M. Hollebon M. Hollands S. Sales, Jnr.
Second Row Tom Winsett, J. Gascoine, Jnr. A. Wimsett, Ted Craddock, J. Butcher
Jnr Stanley Box, R. Prentice

His first home was Spencer's Cottages in Borough Green, and then to one of the two cottages now known as "Stanbredges", and then on to Batt's Cottages at Crouch to be nearer the Mill. Three of his family lived in the Parish of Platt; George Summers at Rose Cottage, Alec Summers at Plough Terrace, Basted, and daughter Rose Bennett at Fir Tree Cottage, Platt, and that was where the old Steeple Jack died in 1912.

When Mr. Monckton died, in his will he left a wish that all the time there was a Summers alive, there is a house for a Summers to live in, and Bossman Tom Summers lived in Monckton Cottages, Bearsted, until he died in 1975.

PLATT MILL

Stanley Box

I was born in Mill Cottage opposite Platt Mill where my father George Box drove a horse-drawn van. When the proprietor George Hide dispensed with the 3 vans, father became mate on the Foden steam-engine, a fascinating machine for us boys, and during school holidays I was allowed to accompany him, sometimes to Wrotham and Borough Green station to collect the sacks of grain, though during the General Strike of 1926, a traction engine belonging to Luke Terry was driven to the London Docks, towing 3 trucks. My father went too and was away for three days, returning black as a chimneysweep.

I left Borough Green school at the age of 14 to work in the Mill, although at 13 I had already worked there after school hours and during holidays. There was a room at the back of the main building which housed the boilers when the Mill was driven by steam, and the tall chimney or shaft was visible from many vantage points. I remember when this shaft was demolished after the fire of 1925 by a gang of men, swinging axes and knocking it down, brick by brick.

Complaints came from neighbours who were disturbed by the Mill engine running all night and day, except between the hours of 6-7 a.m. for maintenance, and when restarted on the main gas supply, it took the pressure away from near-by houses, whose

Platt Mill (before the fire of 1925)

inmates found it difficult to even boil a kettle! At the rear of the Mill was a very deep well from which the water was pumped, and when this pump needed attention, Mr. Gascoine Snr. was lowered down to do the repairs.

The white weather-boarded building on the opposite side of the road, now called 'Cuckoo-Bird', housed the Office and Store for the grain, which was delivered by local farmers, prior to being taken across to the Mill to be ground. The procedure of hoisting up the 2¼ cwt. sacks of grain to the top of the store was as follows: A horse was attached to a rope which went over a pulley at the apex of the building, the horse was led across the road at an angle, owing to the narrow road, and this movement raised the sack from the ground to the door at the top (still visible), then the horse was backed to the store, and the process repeated until all the sacks required were thus delivered. Two kinds of flour were milled: 'Scaling' made from English wheat, used for cakes, buns, puddings, and 'Baker's' for bread only, usually a mixture of Canadian wheat with 10% English.

The foreman, Albert Wimsett, was in charge of the revolving drum; the grain was fed into this drum or funnel, first ground and then refined through 'silks' of different mesh which removed all husks and everything except pure flour. At intervals he would take a handful of this flour, press with a spatula to see if any husks remained, should this happen it was a sign that one of the 'silks' had a hole in it the – machine was then stopped for repairs. The grade of flour was tested by letting a handful pass through his fingers. A part of the Mill was set aside for a remarkable man, Joseph Evans, who was responsible for the up-keep and condition of the sacks.

During the 1914-18 war, Platt Mill was well-known to troops from Exedown Training Camp on their way to France, some would stop and my mother would make cups of tea and 'Nobby' Bance collected money with which to buy the lads buckets of beer, the locals having had warning of the troops' arrival. I well remember when Lord Kitchener came for a review in Addington Parks, troops gathered from all over the South of England. Betty Gibson remembers a beautiful kitchen garden where part of the present Mill building now stands. This was kept immaculate by Mark Hollands; there was a lovely pear tree on the corner, a delight to the children when the fruit was ripe, but not when Mark was around. She also remembers the fire of Dec. 11, 1925, which destroyed two top storeys of the Mill: 'George Bennet's daughter came round to our house and called my father and told us all to get up as there was danger that the petrol tank at the bottom of our garden adjacent to the Mill might explode with the heat.' I was one of the first on the scene, moving lorries away from the fire, an inferno within 15 minutes, since the building contained so much dry timber, the flames reached over the Mill and the roof collapsed. That night was one of the coldest ever remembered, the water had frozen in the hose-pipes, and the road was a sheet of ice. Fire Brigades came from Sevenoaks and Maidstone, one man with icicles on his beard, but there was little hope of saving anything by the time they arrived.

From the Deeds of Platt Mill, made available by the kindness of Mr. Keith Denham of Ford Place, Wrotham Heath, it has been possible to trace the first owner, James Winfield Jull, by an Indenture dated 1880 viz: "All that piece of land lying in the Parish of Wrotham abutting towards the North on the road formerly a Turn-pike road from Maidstone to Sevenoaks; Abutting on the South, land held by Mary Ann Batchelor, and sold by her to John F. Austen, on whose land J. W. Jull erected a Flour Mill and Stables."

The name Mercer occurs in 1885 when J. Jull was declared Bankrupt in 1886, and Authority was given to sell with all fixtures and machinery for £300. Subsequent owners were Frank and Arthur West who paid £2,000 for the Mill, machinery and fixtures in 1891.

Platt Mill 1891

George Hide's name is visible on the front of Platt Mill, but no date of his ownership can be traced so far. He was succeeded by George F. J. Bennett in 1913 and the Mill was sold to Lillico and Son in 1935.

Note. (There is a stone slab under the gable facing East dated 1880) "Dalesfield" where Ronald Evans and his wife Elsie live was built for two of Joseph Evans' sons, Charlie, Albert and their sister Rosie. 'Grandfather' Evans was a remarkable man, a staunch Baptist, father of seven sons and three daughters, he lived in No. 1 Sabraon Villas – Charlie, Albert and Rosie farmed the land called Dalefield, now Greenlands, and kept a flourishing market-garden and a shop in Western Road, Borough Green.

THE BLUE ANCHOR

F. G. Bangay

At sometime (after 1779) altered to The Anchor. Letter dated 13th May 1935 renamed Blue Anchor. Became a full Ale House on 13th May 1954.

1753 - 55	William Luck
1755 - 57	John Hooger
1757	Elizabeth Townsend
1758 - 72	Edward Smith
1772 - 73	William Bance
1773 - 76	Elizabeth Bance (widow)
1776...	William Eversfield
1813...	George Goldsmith
1872 - 75	Hannah Goldsmith (owned by Henry Simmonds of Wrotham)
1903 - 08	Edward Fuller (Henry Simmonds Style & Winch)
1908 - 12	Harriet Fuller
1912 - 34	Frank Hollands,
1934 - 43	John Carter
1943 - 48	Reuben C. Baldwin
1948...	Reuben C. Baldwin
1972	Edward Clark
1973	Peter Rae
1984	F. J. ?Fowles

THE BLUE ANCHOR, PLATT

FORD PLACE, WROTHAM HEATH

Keith Denham

The accompanying illustration of Ford Place is taken from a drawing by Tavener Parry in 1894. This shows the water mill functioning on the far right of the narrow lane at that time between Wrotham Heath and Trottiscliffe.

I am told that this house is a great deal older than its exterior, the Elizabethan North wall and the gables were added towards the end of the 16th century, the last modernisation to the old mediaeval hall which dates back two to three hundred years at least before that.

Hasted calls it "Ford", the American descendants of the 'Clarkes' (who went to America in the 17th century) call it Ford Hall. Old maps call it "Ford", and I think that what remains of it is indeed the Hall of the old Manor House.

When and why it came to be called 'Ford Place' I am unaware, but as Tavener Parry called it "Ford Manor House" in 1894, the word 'Place' must be a recent alteration.

#0053 - 270516 - CO - 210/148/9 - PB - DID1466626